THE BUMPER Book of Kids' JOKES

THE BUMPER Book of Kids' JOKES

ARCTURUS

ARCTURUS
This edition published in 2011 by Arcturus Publishing Limited
26/27 Bickels Yard, 151–153 Bermondsey Street,
London SE1 3HA

ISBN: 978-1-84858-064-0
CH001949EN

Author: Kay Barnham
Editor: Kate Overy
Illustrations: David Mostyn and Quadrum

Supplier 03, Date 0811, Print run 1082

Printed in China

Contents

Get ready to giggle yourself silly!

Are you ready to laugh so hysterically that it feels worse than being tickled? Are you ready for a bumper bundle of side-splitting sniggers? If you like laughter more than a jelly likes to wobble, then read on!

The Bumper Book of Kids' Jokes is jam-packed full of the funniest, silliest, craziest jokes around and there's something for everyone! From knock, knock jokes to classic chuckles, you'll have your friends and family in stitches for hours… days… years! In fact, if you tell enough of these gags, you'll probably be known as the funniest person in the world.

So, take a deep breath and prepare for some of the most eye-wateringly funny jokes ever!

Comedy Creatures

A grizzly bear walked into a café and said,
"I'll have a glass of milk … and a fairy cake."
The waitress looked at him and said,
"What's with the big paws?"

❖

Why don't elephants like playing cards in the jungle?
Because of all the cheetahs.

❖

Did you hear about the crocodile with the camera?
He was snap-happy.

Did you hear about the duck who went to the comedy show?

He quacked up.

❖

How did the puppy stop the DVD?

He used paws.

❖

How do chicks get out of their shells?

They eggs-it.

❖

How do you get down from a camel?

You don't. You get down from a goose.

❖

How do you know if there's an elephant in the fridge?

There are footprints in the custard.

My dog's a blacksmith.
How can you tell?
When I tell him off, he makes a bolt for the door.

❖

What does a cat do when it gets angry?
It goes up the wall.

❖

Why did the pony cough?
Because he was a little hoarse.

❖

What happened when the tortoise collided with the terrapin?
It was a turtle disaster.

❖

One boy says to another boy, "My pet's called Tiny."
"Why?" asks his friend.
"Because he's my newt."

How do you stop a rhinoceros from charging?
Take away its credit cards.

What did the chicken say when it laid a square egg?
Owwww!

❖

What did the frog order at the burger bar?
Some French flies and a Diet Croak.

❖

What did the police officer say when the spider ran down his back?
You're under a vest!

How do you spell "very hungry horse" in four letters?
MTGG.

❖

What's green, cold-blooded and follows the yellow brick road?
The Lizard of Oz.

❖

Why was the glow-worm disappointed?
Because her children weren't very bright.

❖

What do birds eat for breakfast?
Tweetabix.

❖

When can three elephants get under an umbrella and not get wet?
When it isn't raining.

What do whales eat for dinner?
Fish and ships.

❖

What side of a hedgehog is the sharpest?
The outside.

❖

Why do giraffes have such long necks?
Because they have very smelly feet.

What do you call a cat who swallows a duck?
A duck-filled fatty-puss.

What did the grape say when the elephant stepped on him?
Nothing. He just let out a little wine.

❖

What do you call a sleeping bull?
A bulldozer.

❖

Where does the biggest ever spider live?
On the world wide web.

What do you get if you cross a frog with a small dog?
A croaker spaniel.

❖

What do you get if you cross an elephant with a mouse?
Huge holes in the skirting board.

❖

What do you get if you point a hairdryer down a rabbit hole?
Hot cross bunnies.

❖

What do you get if you cross a computer with an elephant?
Loads of memory.

❖

What do you get when an elephant sits on your friend?
A flatmate.

What happens when two snails have a fight?
They slug it out.

❖

What do you give a poorly pig?
Oinkment.

❖

What flies through the jungle singing opera?
The Parrots of Penzance.

❖

What happened when the sheep pen broke?
The sheep had to use a pencil.

❖

What do you call a homeless snail?
A slug.

❖

What fur do you get from a lion?
As fur away as possible.

What do you get if you cross a kangaroo and an elephant?

Very big holes in your garden.

What goes "oo oo"?

A cow with no lips.

❖

What happened to the cat who swallowed a ball of wool?

She had mittens.

❖

What do you get from a nervous cow?

Milkshakes.

What do you call a pony that likes needlework and pottery?

A hobby horse.

What is a cat's favourite colour?

Purrple.

❖

Did you hear about the cat who sucked a lemon?

He was a sourpuss.

❖

What is a cat's favourite party game?

Mewsical chairs.

Why do pet shops always sell out of birds before any other animal?
Because they go cheep.

❖

What is a hedgehog's favourite snack?
Prickled onions.

❖

Where do horses and ponies live?
In the neighbourhood.

❖

How do you get five donkeys in a police car?
Two in the front, two in the back and one on top braying, "hee-haw, hee-haw"!

❖

Why is there no point playing jokes on snakes?
You can't pull their legs.

What should you never do with an angry rhinoceros?
Argue.

❖

What time is it when an elephant sits on your bike?
Time to get a new bike.

❖

What type of cows eat grass?
Lawn moo-ers.

❖

What's a snake's favourite subject?
Hisssstory.

❖

Why do leopards make rubbish thieves?
They are always spotted.

❖

What did one sheep say to the other sheep?
"After ewe."

What goes 99-thump-99-thump-99-thump?

A centipede with a wooden leg.

What noise does an exploding monkey make?

BaBOON!!!

❖

What party game do cows like best?

Moosical chairs.

❖

What should you do if you find a gorilla sleeping in your bed?

Sleep somewhere else!

What's an elephant's favourite game?
Squash.

❖

What's got a hundred legs and can see just as well from both ends?
A centipede with its eyes shut.

❖

What goes "oom oom"?
A cow walking backwards.

What do you call a snake that travels around on the front of a car?
A windscreen viper.

❖

What do you get if you cross a dinosaur with a tea party?
A tyrannosaucer.

❖

What's the difference between a fly and a bird?
A bird can fly but a fly can't bird.

❖

What's the difference between a weasel and a stoat?
A weasel is weasily recognizable and a stoat is stoatily different!

❖

What's the last thing that goes through a fly's mind as it hits the car windscreen?
Its bottom.

What did the pig say when the farmer grabbed him by the tail?
"That's the end of me."

What does a cat rest its head on at night?
A caterpillow.

❖

What's white, furry and smells of peppermint?
A Polo bear.

❖

What's worse than raining cats and dogs?
Hailing taxis.

What do dogs eat at the cinema?
Pupcorn.

❖

Where do insects do their shopping?
In a flea market.

❖

Where do sharks come from?
Finland.

❖

How can you tell that carrots help you see in the dark?
Have you ever seen a rabbit with a torch?

❖

What has three legs and goes "hee-haw"?
A wonky donkey.

Where does a monkey make toast?

Under a gorilla.

❖

Which animal do you find on a legal document?

A seal.

❖

Which animal was out of bounds?

The exhausted kangaroo.

❖

Which bird always sounds out of breath?

A puffin.

❖

Which insect works on a construction site?

A crane fly.

❖

What do you call two birds who have fallen in love?

Tweethearts.

What animal loves a good novel?

A bookworm.

❖

What's grey and has four legs and a trunk?

A mouse going on holiday.

Which reptile would you find relaxing on the sofa?

A lounge lizard.

❖

What do caterpillars do on New Year's Day?

Turn over a new leaf.

What's the healthiest type of insect?
The vitamin bee.

Why are dogs such bad dancers?
They have two left feet.

❖

What do you call a cow with no milk?
An udder failure.

❖

Where do you find an upside-down tortoise?
Where you left it.

Why did the lark use a pair of tongs on her tail feathers?
She thought it was the curly bird who gets the worm.

❖

Why did the lion spit out the clown?
Because he tasted funny.

❖

Why did the tiny terrier puppy bite people's ankles?
He couldn't reach any higher.

❖

Why do birds fly south in the winter?
Because it's too far to walk.

❖

Why do bees have sticky hair?
Because they use honeycombs.

Why do gorillas have big nostrils?
Because they have big fingers!

❖

Why do mice need oiling?
Because they squeak.

❖

What do frogs wear on their feet in summer?
Open-toad sandals.

❖

Why do lions eat raw meat?
Because they don't know how to use ovens.

❖

Where do rabbits go after they're married?
On bunnymoon.

❖

Why do toadstools grow so closely together?
Because they don't need mushroom.

Why were the geese overweight?

They couldn't stop gobbling.

❖

When do squirrels say, "woof woof"?

When they eat acorns and bark.

❖

What weighs a lot and wears glass slippers?

Cinderellephant.

Why did it take the Dalmatian so long to choose a holiday?
He was looking for just the right spot.

❖

Did you hear about the spiders who got married?
They had a huge webbing.

❖

Where do penguins vote?
At the South Poll.

❖

What happened when the frog's car broke down?
It was toad away.

Where do pigs park their cars?
In a car pork.

❖

What kind of bird steals from the rich and gives to the poor?
Robin Hood.

❖

Why did the partridge and the pheasant dress up as clowns?
They were game for a laugh.

❖

What made the fly fly?
The spider spied her.

❖

There are two birds sitting on a perch.
What does one bird say to the other bird?
"Smells of fish."

How do birds see what's behind them?
They look in their wing mirrors.

❖

Why do sheep have woolly coats?
Anoraks don't suit them.

❖

How did the bumblebee contact his friend?
He gave him a buzz.

❖

What name did the snail give to his home?
Michelle.

❖

Why do fish live in salty water?
Pepper makes them sneeze.

❖

Why are wolves like playing cards?
They come in packs.

Where do giraffes go for their lessons?

High school.

What is a fish's favourite type of music?

Bubble rap.

❖

What size are ants' glasses?

They're just specks.

What do you get if you put a mouse in the washing machine?
Squeaky-clean clothes.

❖

What has feathers and writes?
A ballpoint hen.

❖

What do lizards put on their bathroom walls?
Rep-tiles.

❖

A black horse walks into a pub called The Black Horse. "Hi!" says the barman. "Did you know that this pub was named after you?"
"Really?" says the horse. "The pub's called Eric?"

❖

What did the celebrity squirrels sign before they got married?
A pre-nutshell agreement.

Why couldn't the elephant twins go swimming
at the seaside?
Because they only had one pair of trunks between them.

❖

What's the worst kind of cat?
A catastrophe!

❖

Where do you buy baby birds?
At the chickout.

What do penguins do in their spare time?

They chill.

How do you stop a dog from barking in the back seat of a car?

Put it in the front seat.

❖

What do you do with a blue parrot?

Try to cheer it up.

❖

What is a rabbit's favourite type of dancing?

Hip hop.

Two chickens walked into a building the other day.
You would have thought at least one of them would have seen it.

❖

What do you get if you cross an insect and a rabbit?
Bugs Bunny.

❖

Why don't Arctic foxes eat penguins?
They can't get the wrappers off.

❖

Did you hear about the cat who drank ten bowls of water?
He set a new lap record.

❖

Where are elephants found?
They're so huge, it's quite difficult to lose them in the first place.

What noise do porcupines make when they kiss?

Owwwww!

❖

What do you call a donkey with three legs?

A wonkey.

❖

What's brown, furry and has twelve paws?

The Three Bears.

❖

Did you hear about the horse that had six legs?

It had forelegs at the front and two legs at the back.

❖

Why did the Wild West dog limp into the Wild West town?

He came to find the cowboy who shot his paw!

❖

What do birds watch on television?

The feather forecast.

How do rabbits keep their fur tidy?
With hare-spray.

What did the chimpanzee do when he saw a sign saying, "Wet floor"?
He threw water on it.

❖

Did you hear about the cross pig that lost its voice from oinking too much?
It was disgruntled.

What kind of furry animal likes to live underwater?

The Octo-pussy!

How do you catch a totally unique rabbit?

Unique up on it!

❖

How do you catch a tame rabbit?

The tame way. Unique up on it.

❖

Why do Dalmatians never play hide-and-seek?

They are always spotted.

What do cats drink in the desert?

Evaporated milk.

❖

Why does a cow moo?

Because its horns don't work.

❖

How do you catch a squirrel?

Climb up a tree and act like a nut.

❖

Why did the cat become a nurse?

She wanted to be a first-aid kit.

❖

What's a pig's favourite ballet?

Swine Lake.

❖

What do cats eat for breakfast?

Mice Krispies.

What's big, furry and flies?
A hot-air baboon.

❖

What's the most difficult key to turn?
A donkey.

❖

Knock knock!
Who's there?
Wendy.
Wendy who?
Wendy red-red-robin comes bob-bob-bobbin' along!

❖

What happens when ducks fly backwards?
They quack up.

❖

What's the difference between a crazy rabbit and a forged bank note?
One's a mad bunny and the other's bad money.

What do you call a horse that likes cross-stitch and stamp-collecting?

A hobby horse.

❖

How do cows keep up with current affairs?

They watch the Ten O'Clock Moos.

❖

What type of bird digs underground?

A mynah bird.

What do cats put in their drinks?
Mice cubes.

❖

Why should you never trust a whale with your deepest, darkest secrets?
Because they're all blubbermouths.

❖

Which football team came top of the Animal League?
The hedgehogs. They won on points.

What do sharks eat at birthday parties?

Ice cream and jellyfish.

❖

Which fish plays an instrument?

The sea-bass.

❖

Where do tadpoles change into frogs?

In a croakroom.

❖

What do mice do when they get a new home?

They throw a mouse warming party!

❖

What type of biscuits do birds love?

Chocolate-chirrup.

❖

What's a crocodile's favourite card game?

Snap.

What do you call a young goat that learns martial arts?
The Karate Kid.

How do you catch a purple elephant?
In a purple-elephant trap.

❖

How do you catch a green elephant?
Paint it purple and then catch it in a purple-elephant trap.

Which birds are cricketers really scared of?
Ducks.

❖

Where do camels keep their money?
In sand banks.

❖

Why did the silly boy oil the mice?
Because they squeaked.

❖

How do you hire a horse?
Put a brick under each hoof.

❖

Where do beavers keep their money?
In river banks.

❖

Which chocolate bar do dogs like the best?
Kit-kats!

A Shaggy Dog...

A badly dressed, downtrodden man walks into a café and orders a cup of coffee. "Sure," says the waitress, "But I need the money first, you look like you're broke!"

The man answers, "You're right. I haven't got a penny, but if I show you something amazing will you give me a cup?" "It's a deal," says the waitress, intrigued.

So the man reaches into the pocket of his tatty coat and pulls out a mouse. He places the mouse on the counter and hands it a tiny guitar. Immediately the mouse begins to play the teeny tiny guitar with ease, strumming away like a rock star.

"Wow!" says the waitress, "That was amazing, I've never seen anything like it! Here's your free coffee."

The man drinks his coffee and the little mouse disappears back into his coat pocket. "I'll have another," says the man.

"Well, you know the deal," replies the waitress. "Show me another trick and your coffee's on the house!"

The man shrugs his shoulders and reaches into his pocket again. This time he pulls out a frog. He places the frog on the counter and immediately it begins to sing. And what glorious singing! The whole café stops to listen to the tiny frog with the big voice. Suddenly a stranger approaches the scruffy man and says "Hey, how much for the singing frog? I'll give you 200 for him!"

"Sure, he's yours," says the man.

The stranger picks up the frog from the counter, hands over the cash, and skips out of the café, not believing his luck.

"Are you crazy?" says the waitress, "You sold your singing frog for 200, but you could have got millions! He could have made you a fortune!"

"Actually, he's not worth anything," says the man. "The mouse is a great ventriloquist".

What has two humps and is found at the South Pole?

A lost camel.

What do you call a herd of cows with a sense of humour?

Laughing stock.

❖

What's the fastest thing in the sea?

A motor-pike.

What's grey and bounces?
An elephant on a trampoline.

❖

What do you get if you cross an angry sheep with a cross cow?
An animal that's in a baaaaaaaaaaaaaad moooooooooooood.

❖

Why is a hedgehog the most selfish creature in the countryside?
It refuses to share the hedge.

❖

Pretend that you're teetering on top of a towering cliff and a herd of rampaging elephants is thundering towards you. What should you do?
Stop pretending.

❖

Where do turtles go when it rains?
To a shell-ter.

How do you get an elephant into the fridge?
Open the door, shove him in and then shut the door.

❖

What do you get if you cross a porcupine and a giraffe?
A very tall toothbrush.

❖

How do you get a rhino into the fridge?
Open the door, pull out the elephant, shove in the rhino and then shut the door.

❖

Which is the chattiest animal?
A yak.

❖

What did the cheetah say to her cubs when she was teaching them to hunt?
Never step onto the road unless you see a zebra crossing.

What do camels wear when they play hide-and-seek?
Camel-flage.

❖

How can you tell which end of a worm is its head?
Tell it a silly joke and see which end laughs.

❖

Which animal never goes to the hairdresser?
A bald eagle.

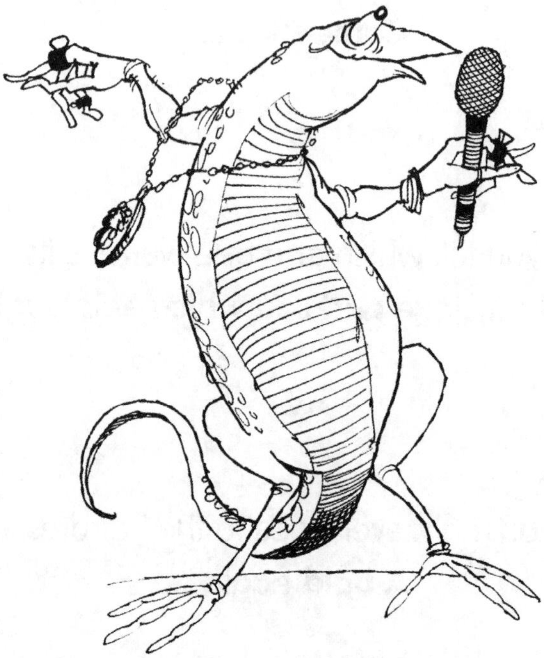

What do you call a singing lizard with a great sense of rhythm?

A rap-tile.

❖

What's the sweetest insect?

A humbug.

❖

What do cats like to watch on television?

The evening mews.

Why did Bo Peep lose her sheep?

She had a crook with her.

❖

What do flies wear on their feet?

Shoos.

❖

What did the Cinderella fish wear to the ball?

A glass flipper!

❖

Which insect is terrific at sums?

An account-ant.

❖

How do you stop moles digging up your garden?

Hide the spades.

❖

Why was the cat scared of the tree?

Because of its bark.

Why wasn't the butterfly invited to the dance?
Because it was a mothball.

❖

Did you hear about the Christmas turkey who tried to escape the roasting pan?
He was foiled.

❖

What is grey, goes bzzzzzzzz and loves to nibble cheese?
A mousequito!

❖

Did you hear about the well-behaved cat?
It was purrfect.

❖

What goes dash-dash-squeak, dash-dash-dash-squeak, dot-dot-dash-squeak, dot-dot-dot-squeak, dot-squeak?
Mouse code.

What do rhinoceroses have that no other animal has?

Baby rhinoceroses.

❖

What's the untidiest insect?

The litterbug.

Which dogs love to have their hair washed?

Shampoodles.

❖

What do sheep do when the weather's hot?

Have a baa-baa-cue.

Did you ever hear of an invisible cat?

No … that's impussible!

❖

How do dinosaurs pass their exams?

With extinction.

❖

What do you call a really spoilt cat?

Pam Purred.

Why did the chicken sit on an axe?

She wanted to hatchet.

❖

What do you get if you cross a caterpillar with a parrot?

A walkie-talkie.

❖

Why are skunks so obedient?

Because they go wherever they're scent.

❖

What did the snake say to his girlfriend after an argument?

Let's hiss and make up!

❖

What's green and jumps a lot?

A frog with hiccups.

❖

What do horses watch to relax?

Saddle-lite TV.

What do polar bears get when they sit on the ice for too long?
Polaroids.

❖

Where do forgetful parrots live?
Polynesia.

❖

What type of joke does a clever duck tell?
A wise quack.

❖

Where do young cows go for their lunch?
A calfeteria.

❖

Which dinosaur has to shelter from the rain?
A Stegosau-rust.

❖

What does a Triceratops sit on?
Its Tricera-bottom.

What's the difference between a boy and a dog?

A boy wears trousers and a dog just pants.

❖

What do you call a Tyrannosaurus rex stuck in quicksand?

Anything you like, he can't chase you.

❖

What do you get if you cross a fairytale character and a pharmacy?

Puss in Boots.

On which day of the year does a cow get a bunch
of flowers and breakfast in bed?

Mudders Day.

What did the fish say when it swam into a concrete wall?

Dam.

❖

What happened when the dog kennels went bust?

They called in the retrievers.

❖

What do you get if you cross a bird with a breakfast cereal?

Shredded Tweet.

Which dinosaurs lie about on the seashore?
Tyrannosaurus-wrecks.

❖

Did you hear about the fish who couldn't stop complaining?
He liked to carp.

❖

Why couldn't the girl have a dog for Christmas?
Because her mum said they were having a turkey like every other year.

❖

What's black and white and black and white and black and white?
A penguin rolling down a hill.

❖

Did you hear about the fight at the fish'n'chip shop?
Two fish were battered.

Where do milkshakes come from?

Riverdancing cows.

❖

What do you get if you cross a kangaroo and a toilet?

A kangaloo.

❖

Which dog uses a punchbag?

A boxer.

❖

Who was the toughest, most ruthless sea creature ever?

Billy the Squid.

❖

Where do cows go on holiday?

Moo York!

❖

Did you hear about the dim glow-worm?

He wasn't very bright.

What do you get if you cross a hen with a bedside clock?
An alarm cluck.

❖

Did you hear about the boy who spilt Spot remover on his dog?
The dog vanished.

❖

Why did the bald man sit a rabbit on his head?
From a distance, they look like hares.

Why couldn't anyone telephone the zoo?
Because the lion was busy.

❖

What do baby snakes play with?
Rattles

❖

How does an elephant get down from a tree?
It sits on a leaf and waits until autumn.

Why don't elephants like playing cards in the jungle?
Because of all the cheetahs.

❖

What do you get if you walk under a cow?
A pat on the head.

❖

Why didn't the prawn like to share?
Because it was a little shellfish.

❖

Why are fish easy to weigh?
They have their own scales.

❖

Did you hear about the little cat sanctuary where poor, abandoned cats go to live?
It was tiny. You couldn't swing a cat in there!

A policeman saw a man walking down the street with a penguin. He told the man to take the penguin to the zoo.

"Good idea," the man said, and off he went.

The next day, the policeman saw the man again. He still had the penguin with him.

"I told you to take that penguin to the zoo," the policeman said.

"I did," the man replied. "He really enjoyed that, so today I'm taking him to the cinema."

Icky Sticky

What's the whiffiest country in the world?
Phew Zealand.

❖

What's the whiffiest city in the world?
Hong Pong.

❖

What's the stickiest and sweetest type of tree?
A tree-cle.

❖

Why did the two-week-old bottle of milk vanish?
It had gone off.

What's the ickiest ice cream flavour?

Lemon and slime.

❖

What did one smelly sheep say to the other smelly sheep?

Ewwwwwwe!

❖

What's loud, sticky and made of phlegm?

A cough sweet.

❖

Did you hear about the eggs who kept throwing themselves at unsuspecting pupils?

They were practical yolkers.

❖

What did the chewing gum say to the shoe?

I'm stuck on you.

What did the cannibals do after the wedding speeches?
They toasted the bride and groom.

❖

What's really icky, really stinky and visits Earth every 76 years?
Halley's vomit.

❖

Did you hear about the American bear who tripped and fell into a blender?
It was a grizzly accident.

❖

What do you get if you boil up 25 cars, three buses and a lorry load of sugar?
Traffic jam.

❖

What do you call a boy standing in the middle of a squishy cowpat?
An in-cow-poop.

What did the Dutch pet-shop owner spread on his croissant?
Hamster jam.

❖

What did the stinky skunk with the terrible memory say when the wind changed direction?
It's all coming back to me now.

Which king had a numb bottom?
The one who was longest on the throne.

What did one egg say to the other egg when it told a joke?
You crack me up.

❖

What type of blood does a pessimist have?
B Negative.

❖

What steps should you take if there's an invasion of giant nose-picking monsters?
Great big ones.

Why did the girl pick her nose at school?
Because she wasn't allowed to pick it at home.

❖

What are big, nutritious and fly together at breakneck speed?
The Red Marrows.

❖

If you divided a treacle tart in half, then in half again
and then you divided each piece into 24 pieces,
what would you get?
Really sticky fingers.

❖

Why did the amoeba cross the microscope?
To get to the other slide.

❖

What's a monster's favourite dessert?
Lice pudding.

Why did the clown throw mud pies at the audience?
It was jest for laughs.

❖

Why was the killer whale sick after gobbling up the vicar?
Because it's hard to keep a good man down.

❖

What's green and has four legs and a trunk?
A seasick elephant.

❖

Why don't cannibals eat clowns?
Because they taste funny.

❖

Why is cutting a huge, creamy slice of Black Forest Gateau the easiest job in the world?
It's a piece of cake.

Why did the handyman have to get false teeth?

Because he kept biting his nails.

❖

What was the fly doing in the gravy?

The breaststroke.

❖

Did you hear about the monster swimmer?

It did the beaststroke!

What did the duck say to the beautician when
she bought lip gloss?
Put it on my bill, please.

❖

Why did the hedgehog cross the road?
To show its guts.

❖

What do you say to a monster with a really runny nose?
Goo away!

Why did the pig go to the amusement arcade?
He wanted to play the slop machine.

❖

What did the monster barman put in all the drinks?
Lice and a slice.

❖

What type of umbrella does a stinky, sweaty monster use on a rainy day?
A wet one.

❖

What's the stinkiest letter of the alphabet?
Ewwwwwwwww.

❖

What do you call a boy with his head down the toilet?
Huey.

A Shaggy Dog...

A family goes on an adventure holiday in the desert. They're having a great time, experiencing new things every day.

One day, they meet a grumpy old camel, who frowns at them all and then spits. "How rude!" says Mum. But Dad laughs it off. "That sort of thing happens all the time in the desert," he says. "It's totally normal."

The next day, the son and daughter spot a group of palm trees in the distance. The family trudges across the dry sand towards it. "How strange to find trees in the desert!" says the son. But Dad laughs it off. "That's an oasis," he says. "You find them all over the desert. It's totally normal."

The following day, the family reaches a town. There, they find a lively and colourful market. The smells are delicious and everyone is looking forward to a hearty meal.

"We'll have some typical regional food," says Dad knowledgeably. At the first stall he asks for meat and vegetables. "Sorry," says the stall holder. "I've only got sherry trifle. There's no meat or veg here." Dad looks disappointed. "Oh," he says.

At the next stall, Dad asks again. "I'd like your best savoury regional speciality," he says. "Sorry, mate," replies the stall holder. "I've got banana and chocolate trifle, but that's it." Dad frowns. "Oh," he says.

And at every single stall they visit, the answer is the same. They all sell gloriously sticky trifles – blueberry trifle, strawberry trifle and orange trifle, but no meat and no veg. Eventually, the family leaves. "And I suppose that's totally normal too?" says Mum. "No," replies Dad. "That's a trifle bazaar."

How do you make a frog float?
...ice cream and a bottle of lemonade. Cheers!

❖

What's red and silly?
A blood clot.

❖

What's brown and sounds like a bell?
Dung!

❖

What do you get if you drop an elephant on a baby butterfly?
A splatterpillar!

❖

What was the snail doing on the M6?
About 20 millimetres an hour.

Why didn't the nose want to go to school?
Because he was always getting picked on.

❖

What do you call a multi-storey pigpen?
A styscraper.

Why are snails' shells so shiny?
They use snail varnish.

What's the difference between bogeys and Brussels sprouts?
Children won't eat Brussels sprouts.

Did you hear about the fly that flew into the sieve at top speed?
It was another fine mesh he'd got himself into.

❖

What did the snail say when he'd climbed onto the tortoise's shell?
Wheeeeeee!

What are a hamster's favourite biscuits?
Hammy dodgers.

❖

What do you give a horse with a tickly throat?
Cough stirrup.

❖

Why are the soles of elephants' feet yellow?
So they can lie upside down and hide in a bowl of custard.

❖

What's the stinkiest animal in the world?
A kangapoo.

❖

Have you ever found an elephant in your bowl of custard?
No? Well, the yellow feet must do the trick, then.

What's sweet, sticky and goes swinging through the jungle?

Tarzipan.

❖

What goes green, red, green, red, green, red?

A toad in a blender.

❖

What colour is poop?

Poople.

❖

What's green, slightly stinky and has a trunk?

A seasick holidaymaker.

❖

What's an ogre's favourite colour?

Slime green.

How do you make a teddy bear go woof?
Put it on a bonfire.

❖

What do you get if you cross an owl with a sewer rat?
A bird that stinks but doesn't give two hoots.

Did you hear about the chicken that told dirty jokes?
It was foul.

What did the speedy squashed tomato say to the slow squashed tomato?

Ketchup!

❖

Why did the beauty contest winner put petit pois in the blender?

She wanted whirled peas.

❖

How many bites can you take out of a whole jam sandwich?

Just the one. Then it's no longer a whole jam sandwich!

❖

What is the most cultured pudding in the world?

Yoghurt.

❖

What do cats like to eat in the summer?

Mice cream.

You can't keep a good joke down...
...especially if it's liquorice-and-Brussels-sprout flavour!

❖

Did you hear about the poorly computer?
It had a nasty virus.

❖

Did you hear about the upside-down man?
His feet smell and his nose runs.

Did you hear the dreadful joke about the pile of manure?
It stinks.

❖

Why did Tigger peer down the toilet?
He was looking for Pooh.

❖

Which famous bear loved to sit on the loo?
Winnie the Pooh.

❖

What's got a bottom at the top?
A toilet.

❖

How do you make a toilet roll?
Push it down a slope.

❖

What did one toilet say to the other toilet?
You look flushed.

Hairy and Scary

What's big, red and eats rocks?
A big, red rock-eater.

❖

What do dirty monsters drink on hot summer days?
Slime cordial.

❖

What happens when a dirty, stinky green monster goes paddling in the Red Sea?
It gets wet.

❖

Why did the weather witch put her wand in the microwave?
She wanted to cast a warm spell.

❖

Did you hear about the police officers who kept watch on the vampire's castle all night?
It was a stake out.

What did the ghost say to his girlfriend?
You look boo-tiful in the moonlight!

❖

What do dirty monsters eat on hot summer days?
Lice lollies.

❖

What do you call a ghost who haunts the town hall?
A night mayor.

Did you hear about the monster comedian?
He was horribly funny.

❖

Why did the ghoul take his suitcase to the funfair?
He wanted to catch the ghost train.

What's evil on the inside and purple on the outside?
A witch dressed as an aubergine.

What do you give a seasick monster?
Plenty of room.

❖

Did you hear about the angry coffin?
It flipped its lid.

❖

Why did the cannibal prefer to live alone?
He was totally fed up with other people.

❖

What was the elephant witch doctor called?
Mumbo Jumbo.

❖

What's as sharp and pointy as one of Dracula's fangs?
His other fang.

What do you call a monster in an aeroplane seat?
Stuck.

❖

Why did the Egyptian mummy call the doctor?
Because of the coffin!

❖

What type of coat does a witch wear in the rain?
A wet one.

❖

There were two apples bobbing in a bucket of water on Halloween. One said, "Crikey, this water's cold."
The other said, "Aaaaargh! A talking apple!"

❖

What did the ghostly commentator use at the Ghouls' Sports Day?
A loudspooker.

How many vampires does it take to screw in a lightbulb?

None. They like the dark.

❖

What do birds sing at Halloween?

Trick or tweet.

❖

How did the doctor bring the ghost back to life?

He took it into the living room.

Where do ghosts go shopping?
Booooooo-tiques!

❖

How do you rid a haunted house of ghosts and ghouls?
With scare freshener.

What spooker player are footballers most afraid of?
The grim keeper.

❖

What type of mistakes do ghosts make?
Boo-boos.

Did you hear about the little ghost with glasses who couldn't scare anyone, no matter how hard he tried?

He was short-frighted.

❖

How do you greet a two-headed monster?

Hello hello!

❖

What's a ghoul's favourite meal?

Spookhetti bolognese.

❖

What do ghosts watch at the haunted theatre?

Romeo and Ghoulliet.

❖

What did the ghostly footballer shout when he scored?

Ghoul!

Did you hear about the fisherman who saw a spook?
It was the ghostguard.

❖

What do witches do when they stay in hotels?
They order broom service.

❖

What did the ghostly teacher say to his puzzled pupils?
Watch the board and I'll go through it again.

❖

Did you hear about the musical ghost?
He wrote haunting melodies.

❖

How do you lock a graveyard at night?
With a skeleton key.

How did the famous ghost publish his life story after he was dead?

It was ghost written.

❖

How do vampires get washed?

In a bloodbath.

❖

What do monsters eat on hot, sunny days?

Eyes cream.

Which is a ghoul's favourite day of the week?
Moanday.

❖

Which is a cannibal's favourite day of the week?
Chewsday.

Which is a spider's favourite day of the week?
Websday.

❖

Which is a vampire's favourite day of the week?
Thirstday.

Which is a ghost's favourite day of the week?
Frightday.

❖

Which is a poltergeist's favourite day of the week?
Scatterday.

❖

Which is a dirty monster's favourite day of the week?
Scumday.

What's a banshee's favourite animal?
The whale.

❖

How do ghosts travel on holiday?
In a scareoplane.

❖

Why do witches never need dictionaries?
Because they're brilliant spellers.

❖

How does a monster with five heads pick his noses?
One at a time.

❖

What pudding do banshees eat at Wimbledon?
Strawberries and scream.

❖

What do you call a werewolf who's spent his life's savings?
Paw.

What do banshees take on holiday?
Sun scream.

❖

What do you get if you cross Tinkerbell with a werewolf?
A hairy fairy.

Where do vampires save money?
In a blood bank!

Where do witches fly?
In the atmosfear.

Why do witches ride broomsticks?
Vacuum cleaners are too heavy.

❖

How did the wizard tell the time?
He checked his wrist witch.

❖

Why do witches eat bacon sandwiches?
They love the cackling.

How did the punk wizard spike his hair?
He used scare gel.

❖

Why didn't the wizard use a pencil to write down his spells?
There was no point.

❖

What's a spook's favourite sweet treat?
Shockolate.

❖

Did you hear about the poltergeist who haunted the china shop?
He was smashing.

❖

Did you hear about the horribly hungry monster who ate a sofa and two armchairs?
He had a three-piece-suite tooth.

What kind of pet does a witch have?

A scaredy cat.

❖

Did you hear about the hairy beast swimming down the rapids?

It was a weir wolf.

❖

What game do banshees play at parties?

Hide and shriek.

❖

Which is a ghost's favourite ice cream?

Boo-berry.

❖

How do you know a vampire has a cold?

He has a coffin fit.

What type of music do ghosts like to dance to?

Haunted house music.

❖

Which is a vampire's favourite ice cream?

Veinilla.

What do Egyptian mummies dance to?

Wrap music.

What do baby ghosts play?
Peekaboo!

❖

Did you hear about the ghostly horse that galloped at midnight?
She was a nightmare.

What do ghosts say before they begin a meal?
Bone appetite!

❖

Where do witches keep their bits and bobs?
In hag bags.

❖

What is Count Dracula's favourite tourist attraction?
The Vampire State Building.

❖

What do you say to a vampire when he gets married?
Coagulations!

❖

What do ghosts take everywhere with them?
Mobile groans.

❖

What do you call a haunted detective story?
Whoooooooodunnit.

Which is a ghost's favourite type of puzzle?
A cryptic crossword.

❖

Who wrote the play about the haunted church?
The crypt writer.

❖

Where did the banshee look up telephone numbers?
In the Yeller Pages.

❖

What do vampires play when it's raining?
Stakes and ladders.

❖

What do vampires sing on New Year's Eve?
Auld Fang Syne.

❖

How do monsters sign their letters?
Best vicious.

What do ghosts wear when they drive anywhere?

A sheetbelt.

❖

What do you call a vampire who falls for practical jokes?

Sucker!

What do French ghosts say in the morning?

Bone-jour.

Did you hear about the identical twin witches?
No one could tell which witch was which.

What did the vampire think of his new false teeth?
They were fangtastic!

Did you hear about the well-behaved witch's cat?
It was purrfect.

What's a ghost's favourite party game?
Musical bumps in the night.

❖

What game do ghosts play at parties?
Musical Scares!

❖

How does a witch feel after long, bumpy journeys?
Broom sick.

❖

What do vampires do for their summer holidays?
They go vamping.

❖

Why don't mummies ever take a break?
Because they never want to unwind.

❖

What is Count Dracula's favourite fruit?
The necktarine.

A Shaggy Dog...

One dark night, Count Dracula is prowling outside a wedding party when he hears a whistling noise and then ...

SPLAT!

A sausage roll catches him on the chin and knocks him backwards. "Ooof!" he says. "I wasn't expecting that."

He continues on his way, looking for unsuspecting victims with lovely necks when ...

BLAT, BLAT!

Two mushroom vol-au-vents hit him, one after the other, messing up his slicked-back black hair.

"What's going on?" he mutters, just before a deluge of yummy missiles heads his way.

KER-SPLAT! SPLOSH! BAM! WHAM! SPLOOSH!

Cheese straws, fairy cakes, vegetable samosas, sandwiches, ice-cream sundaes and finally a huge bowl of sherry trifle bombard him. His scary black cape is covered, his legendary cool is destroyed and his teeth are dripping with strawberry sauce. Dracula is not looking good and he's feeling terrible.

Then suddenly, the truth dawns on him ... "I know who's behind this!" he cries. "It's Buffet the Vampire Slayer!"

Did you hear about the dyslexic demon?
He sold his soul to Santa.

❖

Where do ghosts live?
At the dead end.

❖

Did you hear about the man that used to be a werewolf?
He's all right now-wow-woooooooo!

❖

How did the boy know what the ghost was getting for Christmas?
He felt his presents.

❖

How do you make a witch itch?
Take away the "w"!

Did you hear about the incredibly clever monster?

He was called Frank Einstein.

What did the Loch Ness Monster say to the salmon?

"Long time, no sea."

❖

What do you call a dinosaur that never gives up?

Try-try-try-ceratops.

❖

What type of spells did the spinning witch cast?

Dizzy spells.

How can you tell when there's a giant monster under your bed?
When your nose touches the ceiling.

What do you call a nervous witch?
A twitch.

❖

What do you call a skeleton who can't be bothered to get out of bed?
Lazy bones.

Why don't witches get sunburnt?
They use suntan potion.

❖

Did you hear about the overweight witch?
She went to Weight Witches.

❖

Did you hear about the witch's breakfast cereal?
It went snap, cackle and pop.

❖

What do trainee witches do at school?
Spelling tests.

❖

What do you do with a blue monster?
Try to cheer it up.

❖

Why couldn't the frightened archer hit the target?
Because his arrows were all in a quiver.

What is a witch's favourite fruit?
Wartermelon.

❖

What do cannibals say when they fall out of love?
I'm sorry but I just 'ate you.

❖

What's the spookiest sweet in the world?
Marshmalloween.

❖

Who lights up a haunted house?
The lights witch.

❖

Why couldn't the ghost order a vodka at the bar?
They didn't serve spirits.

❖

Who cleans a haunted school?
A scaretaker.

What does the headless horseman ride?

A night mare.

❖

Did you hear about the witch's enormous mixing pot?

It was called Ron.

❖

Where do you find giant snails?

At the end of giants' fingers.

❖

What do you call a dinosaur wearing a blindfold?

Doyouthinkhesaurus.

What does a wet-weather witch do?

She forecasts rainy spells.

Why didn't the witch wear a flat cap?

There was no point.

❖

What's the scariest player on a football team?

The ghoulie.

❖

I have a large, hooked nose, three eyes and cabbages for ears. What am I?

Really ugly.

What do cannibals eat on toast?

Baked beings.

❖

What do you do with a green monster?

Wait until it's ripe.

❖

What do you get from a ghost cow?

Evaporated milk.

❖

What do you get when dinosaurs crash their cars?

Tyrannosaurus wrecks.

❖

What happened when Dracula swallowed a sheep?

He felt baaaaaaaaaaaad.

❖

What happened when the ghosts went on strike?

A skeleton staff took over.

Where do ghosts swim?
In the Dead Sea.

❖

Why are ghosts dreadful liars?
You can always see through them.

❖

Why are graveyards never deserted?
There's always somebody there.

❖

Why couldn't the skeleton go to the disco?
He had no body to dance with.

❖

Why do demons and ghouls get on so well?
Because demons are a ghoul's best friend.

❖

What is wicked on the inside and green and knobbly on the outside?
A witch dressed as an avocado.

What type of coffee does a vampire drink?

De-coffin-ated.

❖

What goes "WOO-HA-HA" THUMP?

A monster laughing his head off.

❖

What's the best way to speak to a scary monster?

Long-distance.

❖

Why do dragons sleep during the day?

So they can fight knights.

What's Dracula's favourite soup?

Scream of mushroom.

❖

What sport do vampires play?

Batminton.

❖

How do witches make their own hair stand on end?

With scarespray.

How do you describe a smelly witch with heaps of gold stashed away in her cauldron?

Stinking witch.

How does a monster count to 17?
On his fingers!

❖

Where do ghouls go swimming?
Lake Eerie.

❖

What do you call a haunted policeman?
Inspectre.

❖

How do ghosts send letters overseas?
By scaremail.

❖

How do ghosts begin business letters?
"Tomb it may concern…"

❖

What do you call a vampire that lives in the kitchen drawer?
Count Spatula.

What do you get when a dinosaur sneezes?
Out of the way!

❖

Which monster is green and stroppy?
The Incredible Sulk.

❖

What is the Abominable Snowman's favourite meal?
Spag-yeti.

❖

Did you hear about the banshee who wanted to be an actress?
She did a scream test.

❖

Did you hear about the vampire who went to the fast-food restaurant?
He wanted a quick bite.

❖

What has handles and flies?
A witch in a dustbin.

How do ghouls make their fortunes?

They buy and sell scares on the Shock Exchange.

❖

What's Count Dracula's second favourite fruit?

A blood orange.

❖

Which monster can't help picking his nose?

The bogeyman.

❖

How do skeletons keep in touch?

They use mobile bones.

What kind of dog does a vampire own?
A bloodhound.

Why did the car stop when it saw the headless monster?
It had a nervous breakdown.

❖

What's the most terrifying ride at the funfair?
The rollerghoster.

❖

What do ghosts and ghouls say to each other at sunset?
Good moaning!

Which monster is the best dancer?
The boogieman.

❖

What do vampires do at eleven o'clock every night?
They have a coffin break.

❖

What do you call a chicken that goes bump in the night?
A poultrygeist.

❖

Did you hear about the lazy skeleton?
He was bone idle.

❖

Where do you find a cemetery?
In the dead centre of town.

❖

Why don't skeletons play music in churches?
They have no organs.

What do you call an unidentified wizard on a broomstick?
A flying sorcerer.

❖

What did the archaeologist shout when he opened the tomb?
"Mummy!"

❖

What happened when the two ghosts bumped into each other in the dark alley?
It was love at first fright.

❖

Who won the monsters' beauty contest?
No one.

What type of ballroom dancing does a vampire do best?

The fango.

❖

What's a monster's favourite party game?

Swallow the leader.

What do vegetarian cannibals eat?

Swedes.

❖

Where do stinky witches get washed?

In a hubble bubble bath.

What type of music do demons listen to?
Soul music.

❖

Why should witches never lose their tempers while they're zooming around on a broomstick?
They would fly off the handle.

❖

What do really ugly monsters buy at the local shop?
Grosseries.

❖

What do birds play at Hallowe'en?
Trick or tweeting.

Spoof Stuff

Films They Never Made

Doctor Dolotsandlots

The man who wouldn't stop talking to the animals, even when they REALLY wanted him to shut up

❖

The Sound of Moosic

A bovine epic, featuring the most melodic cows in Austria

Nanny McPhee-ew

The story of a Scottish nanny who ran a marathon

❖

Monsters' Ink

Monsters' pens don't work without it

❖

Scooby Don't

The story of a dog who never has any adventures

❖

51 Dalmations

The abridged version

❖

The Jingle Book

A Christmassy film of sleighbells

❖

Harry Potter and the Goblet of Clay

One boy's mission to master the art of pottery

What the film was REALLY about

Star Wars

The battle of the TV celebrities

❖

Grease

A sticky tale of solidified chip fat

❖

Jurassic Park

One palaeontologist's historic discovery of a prehistoric playground

❖

Losing Nemo

Oops, there he goes again

❖

Alice in Sunderland

Alice takes a trip to the north-east of England

Stinkerbell

The naughtiest – and smelliest – fairy ever

❖

Nice Age

A bunch of prehistoric creatures have a lovely time, with no trouble at all from snow, ice or predators

❖

Down

The eagerly awaited sequel to "Up"

❖

The Polar Express

The story of the number-one Arctic newspaper

Almost Famous

Walt Sing
The ballroom dancing star from Vienna

❖

Anna Rack
The really drippy inventor of the waterproof coat

❖

I. M. Ansome
The best looking man...

Megan Stuffup
The fairytale writer

❖

Noah Zark
The number-one shipbuilder

❖

Laura Norder
The policewoman who arrested the most people ever

❖

X L Entmarks
The best exam-passer ever

❖

Lou Pole
The world-class barrister

Laughter Library

Dangerous Waters
by Gail Force

❖

The Yellow Sea
by I. P. Freely

❖

How to Speak Like a Pirate
by I. I. Jim Lad

❖

Fly Fishing
by Rod Enreel

Back of the Net
by E. Shoots & E. Scores

❖

How to Play Leapfrog
by Ben Dover

❖

Gymnast Fashion
by Leah Tard

❖

Kapow!
by Marsha Lartz

❖

Navel Gazing
by Belle E. Button

❖

Whodunnit?
by Howard I. Know

Stinking Rich
by Iona Castle

❖

The Final Act
by Kurt N Call

❖

The Perfect Accompaniment to a Cup of Tea
by Duncan Biskit

❖

The Unwanted Guest
by Al B Back

❖

A Complete History of Manmade Fabrics
by Polly S Terr

❖

How to Pack Your Trunk
by Ellie Fant

Top Tips for Christmas Kisses

by Miss L Tow

❖

Smells at Bay

by Lydia Dustbin

My Dad's Lost His Car Keys Again

by Fran Tick

The Worst Animal Jokes Ever
by Terry Bull

❖

The Rat Catcher
by X. Terminate

❖

The Ghostspotters' Guide
by R. U. A. Spook

❖

They're Devilishly Handsome
by D. Munns

❖

How to Scare Yourself Silly
by Herr Raising-Pranks

❖

The Indecisive Vampire
by Woody Bite

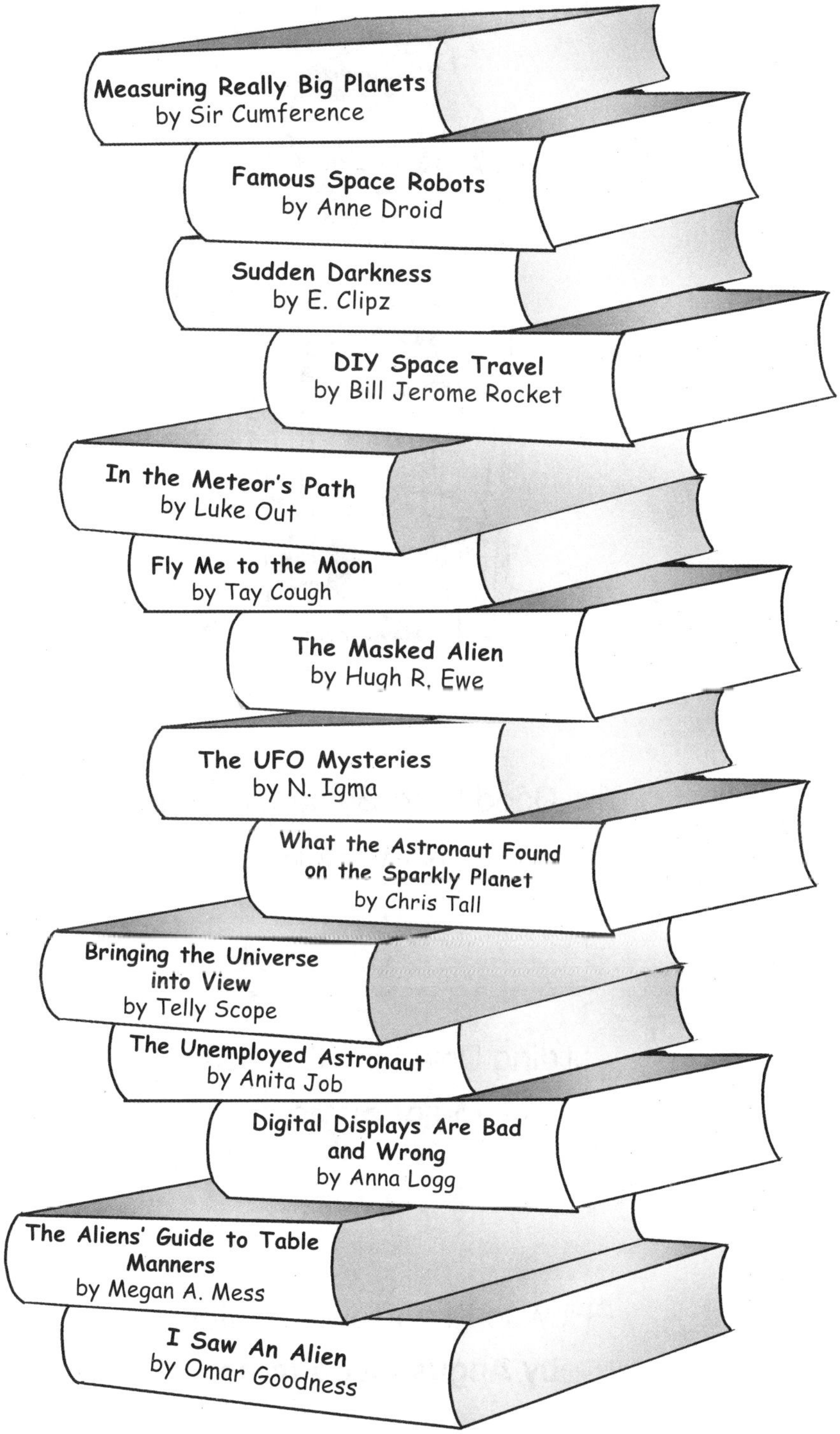
Measuring Really Big Planets by Sir Cumference
Famous Space Robots by Anne Droid
Sudden Darkness by E. Clipz
DIY Space Travel by Bill Jerome Rocket
In the Meteor's Path by Luke Out
Fly Me to the Moon by Tay Cough
The Masked Alien by Hugh R. Ewe
The UFO Mysteries by N. Igma
What the Astronaut Found on the Sparkly Planet by Chris Tall
Bringing the Universe into View by Telly Scope
The Unemployed Astronaut by Anita Job
Digital Displays Are Bad and Wrong by Anna Logg
The Aliens' Guide to Table Manners by Megan A. Mess
I Saw An Alien by Omar Goodness

The Good Food Guide for Dogs
by Nora Bone

❖

Sliding Down the Bannister
by Major Bumsore

❖

How to Keep Your Hall Tidy
by Angus McCoatupp

I Give Up
by Sir N Derr

❖

Never Give Up
by Percy Vere

❖

All the Fun of the Fair
by Tom Bowler

❖

The Girl Who Couldn't Stop Complaining
by Mona Lott

❖

The Pros and Cons of Fighting
by Warren Peas

❖

I Fell Down a Rabbit Hole
by Alyson Wonderland

The Most Popular Chinese Dishes of All Time
by Chris P Duck

❖

The Polite Policemen
by Eve Ninall

❖

The Generous Millionaire
by Benny Factor

❖

The Roman Who Was Sacked From His Construction Job
by Ben Dinroad

❖

The Amazing Vanishing Woman
by Fay de Way

❖

Perfect Place to Keep All Your Pants
by Chester Drawers

When the Wind Blows
by Russell Ingleaves

❖

Classic Fiction
by Warren Peace

❖

What Makes Lightbulbs Glow?
By Elektra City

❖

Is There Life on Mars?
by Howard Dino

The Man Who Couldn't Stop
by Juan Moore-Thyme

❖

How To Keep A House Warm in Winter
by Ray D. A. Torr

❖

What To Do When The Sand's Too Hot To Walk On
by Lee Ping

❖

The Day Father Christmas Got Rid of His Beard
by Klaus Shave

The Survivors' Guide to Escaping from a Sinking Ship
by Mandy Lifeboats

❖

Putting One Brick On Top Of Another In A Really Neat Way
by Bill Ding

❖

The Secret of Mega-Speedy Cookery
by Mike Rowave

❖

How To Fit A Safety Net
by Justin Case

❖

Over the Cliff
by Hugo First

❖

Pickling Vegetables
by B. Troot

Cooking French Food
by Sue Flay

❖

Too Many Beans
by Wynn D. Bottom

Grub's Up
by Carmen Gettit

❖

What the Diner found on His Side Plate
by Roland Butter

❖

The Enormous Sum
by Adam Upp

❖

Top of the Class
by Jeanie Yuss

❖

I Nearly Missed the School Bus
by Justin Thyme

❖

The Eager Pupil
by I. Wanda Know

I Love To Sing Extremely Loudly And Slightly Off-Key
In Public
by Carrie Oakey

❖

The Dizziest Dances of All Time
by Ed Banger

Disaster at Sea!
By May Day

❖

That's Just Not Funny Any More
by Bjorn de Joke

❖

Tatty Old Furniture
by Anne Teak

❖

How to Think Really Deeply
by Phil Ossofy

❖

Gone Fishing
by Courtney Biggins

❖

The World's Cheekiest Monkeys
by Bob Boone

Books They Never Wrote

War and Peas

The Battle of the Small Green Vegetables

❖

Jane Air

The Nineteenth-Century Romantic Heroine who Suffered from Terrible Wind

❖

Grimm's Furry Tales

or Cute and Cuddly Classics

The Sword in the Scone

or When King Arthur Discovered that He Needed Contact Lenses

❖

Charlotte's World Wide Web

or The Spider Who Got Broadband

❖

Just Sew Stories

A Collection of Needlework and Embroidery Fables

❖

James and the Giant Pitch

A Marvellous Football Fable

❖

Harry Potter and the Deathly Halitosis

A teenage boy's struggle with chronic bad breath.

What the Book was REALLY about

The Wonderful Wizard of Oz
or The Fantastic Magician from Down Under

❖

Little Red Riding Hood
or The Coat that Shrank in the Wash

❖

The Night Before Christmas
or What Happened on the Twenty Fourth of December

❖

Five Children and IT
or A Group of Kids Learn Computer Skills

❖

Little Women
or Four Sisters All Under Five Feet Tall

The Jungle Book
or Survival Tips for Young Explorers

❖

Where the Wild Things Are
or Check Under Your Bed Before you go to Sleep

❖

The Cat in the Hat
or The Magician who Misplaced his Rabbit

Ooops, My Trousers Fell Down!
by Lucy Lastick

❖

Casual Beach Footwear
by Philippe Fillop

❖

The Deadliest Jokes Ever
by Di Laffing

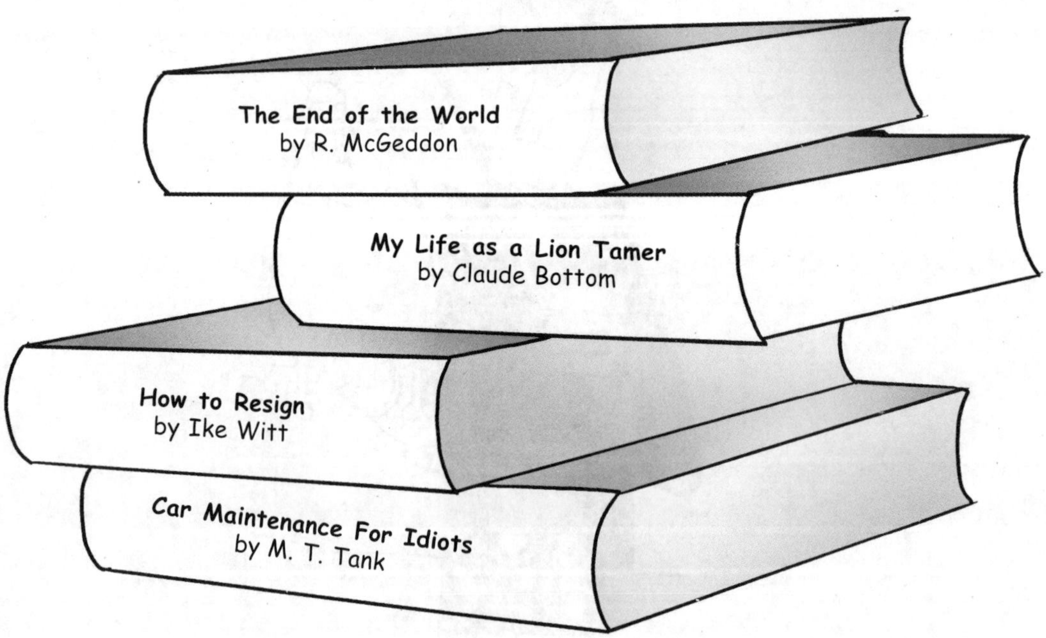

Medical Mischief

Doctor, doctor, how can I cure flat feet?

With a foot pump.

❖

Doctor, doctor, my nose is running.

No, I think you'll find it's snot.

❖

Doctor, doctor, I feel like a dog!

Sit!

❖

Doctor, doctor, I feel like a pack of cards.

I'll deal with you later.

❖

Doctor, doctor, I feel like a pair of curtains.

Well, pull yourself together, then.

❖

Doctor, doctor, I feel like a snooker ball.

Go to the end of the queue.

Doctor, doctor, can you get rid of my spots?
I never make rash promises.

❖

Doctor, doctor, can you give me something for my liver?
How about some nice fried onions?

❖

Doctor, doctor, I keep seeing a ladybird doing pirouettes.
Oh, that's just a bug that's going round.

Doctor, doctor, I think I'm a clock!
Don't get wound up about it.

Doctor, doctor, I feel like a witch's hat.
I see your point.

❖

Doctor, doctor, I think I'm a wastepaper bin.
Don't talk rubbish.

❖

Doctor, doctor, I think I'm an elastic band!
Stretch yourself out on the couch then.

Doctor, doctor, I haven't slept for days!
Why not?
Because I sleep at night!

❖

Doctor, doctor, I keep getting sharp stabbing pains in my eye when I drink tea!
Take the spoon out of the cup then.

❖

Doctor, doctor, I keep seeing double.
Take a seat, please.
Which one?

❖

Doctor, doctor, I keep thinking I'm a bridge.
What's come over you?
Six cars, three trucks and a double-decker bus.

❖

Doctor, doctor, I keep thinking I'm a goat.
How long has this been going on for?
Since I was a kid.

❖

Doctor, doctor, people keep ignoring me.
Next!

Doctor, doctor, I keep thinking I'm a bell.
Take these pills. If they don't work, give me a ring.

❖

Doctor, doctor, I have a fish bone stuck in my throat!
Are you choking?
No, I'm serious!

❖

Doctor, doctor, I think I'm a leech.
Get out of here, sucker!

❖

Doctor, doctor, I've eaten three black snooker balls and two pink ones and I feel dreadful!
I'm not surprised. You aren't eating enough greens.

❖

Doctor, doctor, can you help me out?
Certainly, put your arm through mine and I'll escort you off the premises.

Doctor, doctor, I think I'm a frog.
Hop it!

Doctor, doctor, I've only got 59 seconds to live!
I'll see you in a minute.

❖

Doctor, doctor, I'm terrified of squirrels!
You must be nuts.

❖

Doctor, doctor, I've just swallowed a clock!
Don't panic, there's no cause for alarm.

A Shaggy Dog...

A girl is on her way to school when an enormous stag beetle jumps onto the pavement in front of her. "Ner-ner-ner-ner-ner!" it shouts. "You smell!"

The girl watches as the stag beetle scuttles off. "That wasn't very nice," she says to herself and carries on towards school.

When she gets there, everyone is talking about the huge insect. "It told me I was fat!" says one boy. "It called me specky-four-eyes!" says another. "Pay no attention." says the teacher.

On the way home from school, the girl keeps a lookout for the stag beetle. She has no desire to be insulted again. But the beetle finds her – and this time it calls her "a blithering idiot" and then throws a water balloon at her. The girl is drenched with water and so upset that when she gets home, her mother decides to take her to see the doctor.

The doctor listens to everything, occasionally nods his head and at last he speaks.

"Hmmm," he says. "I did hear that there was a nasty bug going around."

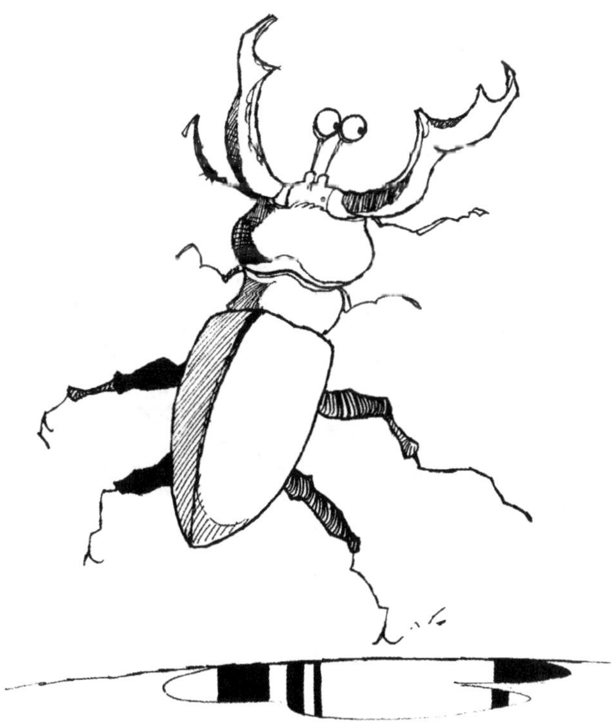

Doctor, doctor, I think I need glasses.
I think you do. This is a delicatessen.

❖

Doctor, doctor, I can't stop stealing things!
Take these pills. If they don't work, get me a plasma TV and a bag of gold bullion.

❖

Why did the boy creep past the medical cabinet?
He didn't want to disturb the sleeping pills.

Doctor, doctor, have you got anything for a terrible headache?
Yes, bash yourself twice on the head with this mallet.

❖

Doctor, doctor, I feel like a box of cheesy biscuits.
You're crackers!

❖

Doctor, doctor, I'm becoming invisible.
Yes, I can see that you're not all there.

❖

Doctor, doctor, I keep thinking I'm a caterpillar.
You'll soon change.

❖

Doctor, doctor, I can't get to sleep at night.
Sit right on the edge of the bed and you'll soon drop off.

❖

Doctor, doctor, I keep thinking I'm a desk.
You're just letting things get on top of you.

Doctor, doctor, I keep thinking I'm an adder.
Grab this calculator and help me with my accounts then.

❖

Doctor, doctor, I smell like fish.
You poor sole.

❖

Doctor, doctor, I can't help frightening people.
Argggghhhhhh!

❖

Doctor, doctor, I have a big, juicy strawberry on my head.
I'll give you some cream for that.

❖

Doctor, doctor, I think I'm suffering from a bad case of déjà vu.
I've seen you before.

❖

Doctor, doctor, what can you give me for wind?
Here's a kite.

Doctor, doctor, will I be able to play the tin whistle after the operation?

Yes, of course.

Excellent! I've never been able to play it before!

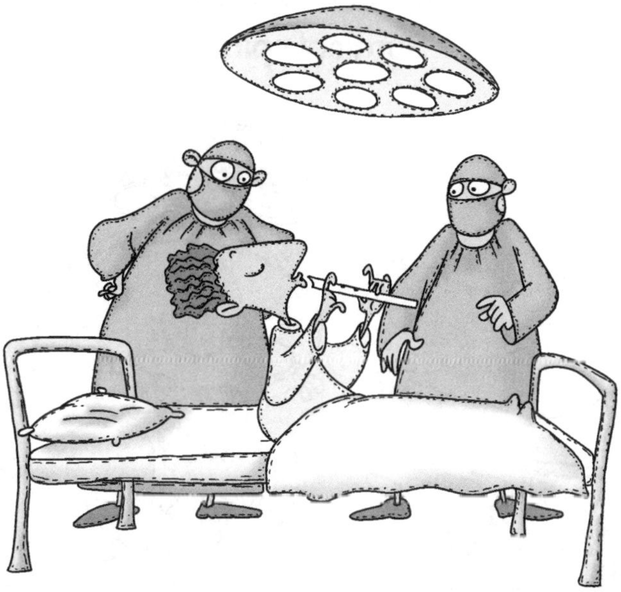

Doctor, doctor, I'm a compulsive thief!

You'd better take something for that.

❖

Doctor, doctor, I keep thinking I'm a wigwam and then a teepee.

Hmmm. You're definitely two tents.

Doctor, doctor, I keep thinking I'm a plant.

We must get to the root of this problem.

❖

Which ghosts haunt operating theatres?

Surgical spirits.

Doctor, doctor, I've swallowed a roll of film!

Let's hope nothing serious develops.

❖

Doctor, doctor, how can I stop my nose from running?

Trip it up.

Doctor, doctor, I keep thinking I'm a boa constrictor.
You can't get round me, you know.

❖

Doctor, doctor, my snoring's keeping me awake.
Well, sleep in another room!

❖

How did the patient get to the doctor so quickly?
He flu.

❖

What did one eye say to the other eye?
Between you and me, something smells.

❖

Doctor, doctor, I think I'm a strawberry.
Hmmm... You're in a jam.

❖

Doctor, doctor, I've swallowed my pen!
Don't worry, you can borrow mine.

Why are false teeth like stars?
They come out at night.

❖

How do dentists check crocodiles' teeth?
Very carefully.

❖

What did the tiger eat after he'd had all his teeth pulled out?
The dentist.

❖

Where do dentists go boating?
Up root canals.

❖

Why did the boy wear a belt on his teeth?
He couldn't find his braces.

❖

Doctor, doctor, I feel like a bee.
Buzz off!

Why did the queen go to the dentist?

To get her teeth crowned.

What type of fish carries out operations?

A sturgeon.

❖

What did the dentist say when she stood up in front of the judge?

"I swear to tell the tooth, the whole tooth and nothing but the tooth."

❖

If you broke your leg in two places what would you do?

Never go back to those two places!

What's the most tuneful bone?
The trom-bone.

❖

What do you call a couple of doctors?
A pair-a-medics.

❖

What happens when dentists remove braces?
Their trousers fall down.

❖

Doctor, doctor, I feel like a spoon.
Sit down and don't stir!

❖

Doctor, doctor, I think I've got woodworm.
How boring for you!

School Shockers

Why was the school cook arrested?
Because she beat the eggs and whipped the cream.

❖

Did you hear about the cowboy who helped run the school?
He was the deputy head.

❖

How did the Vikings send secret messages during lessons?
By Norse Code.

❖

What do elves do after school?
Gnomework.

❖

What did the set square say to the protractor?
Take me to your ruler.

❖

How do you fix a broken tuba?
With a tubaglue.

What was the dog awarded when he left university?

A pedigree.

What did the computer eat for dinner?

A byte.

❖

Why did the school cook pour petrol into his cake mix?

He wanted to make it light.

❖

Why do learner witches need dictionaries?

They can't spell.

If two's company and three's a crowd,
then what are four and five?
Nine.

❖

What runs but never walks, has a mouth but never talks,
has a bed but never sleeps?
A river.

❖

Which snake is good at sums?
An adder.

If the red house was made of red bricks and the brown house was made of brown bricks, what was the green house made of?
Glass.

❖

Which is fastest, cold or heat?
Heat. You can catch a cold.

❖

Did you hear about the cannibal that was expelled from school?
He was buttering up the teachers.

❖

If I slice three pears into five pieces, what have I got?
Really sticky fingers.

❖

Is it easier to write with your right hand or your left hand?
Neither. It's easier to write with a pen.

What did the enormous computer eat for dinner?
A megabyte!

❖

What do IT teachers eat for dinner?
Chips.

❖

What do really tiny IT teachers eat for dinner?
Microchips.

❖

What do you call a Roman emperor with a cold?
Julius Sneezer.

❖

What do you get if you cross a vampire and a teacher?
Blood tests.

❖

What kind of lighting did Noah use for his ark?
Floodlights.

What is an insect's best subject at school?

Mothematics.

❖

What foreign language are birds really good at?

Portugeese.

❖

What did the headteacher say to the naughty egg?

"You're eggspelled."

What kind of meals do geometry teachers enjoy?
Square meals.

❖

What's the fruitiest lesson at school?
History. It's full of dates.

❖

What's the longest sentence ever?
Life imprisonment.

❖

What did the 0 say to the 8?
"Cool belt."

❖

Where do bad spellers look up words?
In a dickshunerry.

❖

Where was the Magna Carta signed?
At the bottom.

Which tree has square roots?

A geometry.

❖

What's the longest word in the world?

"Smiles," because there's a mile between the first letter and the last.

❖

Why did the girl go to night school?

Because she wanted to learn to read in the dark.

Why was Elizabeth I buried at Westminster Abbey?
Because she was dead.

❖

Why did the teacher wear sunglasses?
Because his class was so bright.

What do you get if you divide the circumference of a pumpkin by its diameter?
Pumpkin pi.

❖

Why did the girl stare at the orange juice carton?
Because it said "concentrate" on the label.

Why did the Romans build straight roads?
So they didn't go round the bend.

❖

Where do ghosts do their homework?
In an exorcise book.

❖

Why is Europe like a dirty frying pan?
Because it has Greece at the bottom.

❖

Why is six scared of seven?
Because seven ate nine.

❖

What comes before 11?
The postman.

❖

Why don't cannibals like the sum four plus four?
Because they get eight.

What's purple and burns?
The Grape Fire of London.

❖

Did you hear about the schoolboy whose mummy asked him why he took his pencil to bed?
He said, "Because you told me to draw the curtains."

❖

Why was the cross-eyed teacher's class rioting?
She couldn't control her pupils.

Why did the pupil think the teacher had a crush on him?
She put Xs all over his homework.

❖

Which animal is the best at maths?
Rabbits. They can multiply really quickly.

❖

Where did Noah keep his oldest bees?
In the ark hive.

❖

What was the dentist's favourite subject at school?
Flossophy.

❖

Why was the maths textbook miserable?
It had too many problems.

❖

Which building always has the most storeys?
A library.

A Shaggy Dog...

There was once an inflatable boy who lived in an inflatable world. He had an inflatable mum and an inflatable dad, who puffed up with pride whenever they saw him.

The inflatable boy went to an inflatable school and had his lessons in an inflatable classroom, with his inflatable friends. He had an inflatable teacher, who spouted a lot of hot air during lessons, but otherwise told the inflatable boy lots of very useful facts.

One unfortunate day, the inflatable boy was pinning up a poster on the non-inflatable noticeboard. But he slipped and punctured the wall of the classroom. Slowly, and with a great

hisssssss, the room began to deflate. The inflatable teacher rushed over to take the drawing pin off the boy, but there was a loud "pop" and she began to deflate.

"Oh no!" cried the inflatable boy. He grabbed the pin back, but in the process accidentally pricked his finger. Hisssssss. He began to deflate too!

After a visit to the inflatable first-aider, the inflatable boy and the inflatable teacher were repaired, but the entire school was now in a great airless heap on the floor.

The inflatable headmaster called the inflatable boy to what remained of his office. "I hope you're ashamed of yourself," the headmaster said crossly. "You've let the school down. You've let your teacher down. But worst of all, you've let yourself down."

Why didn't the girl go to the end of the school dinner queue?
There was already somebody there.

❖

Where was Queen Elizabeth II crowned?
On her head.

❖

What did Henry VIII become on his 21st birthday?
A year older.

❖

Did you hear about the chick that misbehaved in all its lessons?
It was eggspelled!

❖

Who invented fractions?
Henry the Eighth.

❖

Why was Rome built at night?
Because it wasn't built in a day.

Why was the Music teacher locked out of his classroom?

The keys were on the piano.

Which tools come in handy during a maths lesson?

Multi-pliers.

❖

What do we do with crude oil?

Teach it good manners.

❖

Why did the school cook get a shock?

He stepped on a teacake and a currant went up his leg.

Why was the broom late for school?

It overswept.

Why was the computer coughing and sneezing and sniffing?

Because it had a virus.

❖

What was Camelot famous for?

Its knight life.

❖

If you cut a potato into sixteenths, what will you have?

Chips.

What's the capital of Peru?

P.

❖

Who invented King Arthur's round table?

Sir Cumference.

❖

Which month has 28 days?

All of them.

❖

What is adding?

It's the noise a doorbell makes.

❖

Why did the teacher put the lights on?

Because the class was dim.

❖

What's a maths teacher's favourite meal?

Pi.

Why did Henry VIII have so many wives?

He liked to chop and change.

❖

What do elves learn at school?

The elf-abet.

❖

Which word is always spelt incorrectly?

Incorrectly.

❖

What are you going to be when you leave school?

Older.

❖

Which are the coldest sort of triangles?

Ice-soceles.

❖

How do bees get to school?

On the buzz.

Why did the teacher jump into the swimming pool?
She wanted to test the water.

What's the fastest way to double your money?
Fold it in half.

❖

Where does success come before work?
In a dictionary.

❖

Why did one pencil tell the other pencil
that it looked old and worn out?
Because it was blunt.

Which word in the dictionary is always spelt wrongly?

Wrongly.

❖

Why did the maths teacher tell her student that he was average.

She was being mean.

❖

Teacher: Can you think of a sentence using the word "fascinate"?

Pupil: My grandad has a shirt with ten buttons down the front, but he has such a big tummy that he can only fascinate.

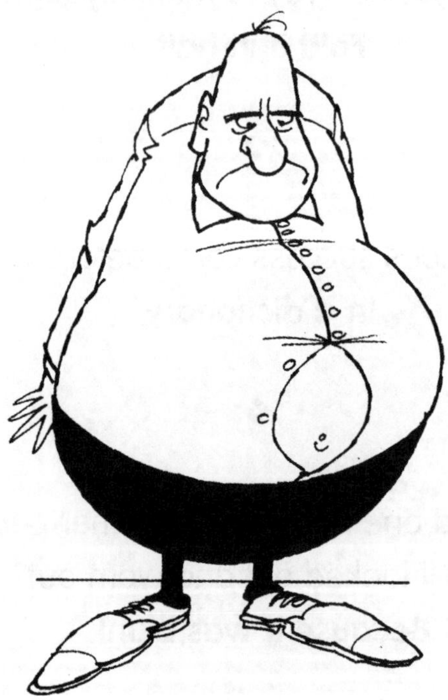

Which famous brothers didn't invent the aeroplane?

The Wrong brothers.

❖

Did you hear about the schoolboy who dreamt he wrote The Lord of the Rings?

He was Tolkien in his sleep.

❖

Which tables don't they teach you in Maths?

Dinner tables.

❖

When is an exam paper not an exam paper?

When it's turned in to the examiner.

❖

What did one maths textbook say to the other maths textbook?

I've got problems.

❖

Why was it so easy for Sherlock Holmes to learn his ABCs?

Because it was LMN-try.

What is a cow's favourite lesson?
Moo-sic.

❖

Have you heard the joke about the blunt pencil?
Sorry, there's no point.

❖

Which schoolbag is always tired?
A knapsack.

❖

How do pupils get straight As?
By using a ruler.

❖

What is a polygon?
A dead parrot.

❖

Why was the school girl excited?
Because the teacher had told her to wait there for the present.

Classic Chuckles

Why did the chicken cross the road?
To get to the other side.

Why did the pterodactyl cross the road?
Because chickens didn't exist then.

❖

What did the farmer use to repair his shirt?
A cabbage patch.

❖

Why did Captain Hook cross the road?
To get to the second hand shop.

Why did the chicken cross the playground?
To get to the other slide.

❖

Why did the chicken cross the road, jump in a muddy ditch and cross back over the road again?
Because he was a dirty double-crosser.

❖

How many chickens does it take to change a lightbulb?
None, they're all too busy crossing the road.

❖

A girl walks into a shop and says,
"I'd like to buy a wasp, please."
"But we don't sell any wasps," says the shopkeeper.
"That's funny," says the girl.
"You have one in your window."

❖

How many babysitters does it take to change a lightbulb?
None. Lightbulbs don't wear nappies.

How can you keep a wet dog from smelling?

Hold its nose.

❖

What kind of a wig can hear?

An earwig.

❖

How many shop assistants does it take to change a lightbulb?

One, as long as you have the receipt.

❖

Knock knock.
Who's there?
Cash.
Cash who?
No, thanks. I prefer walnuts.

❖

Knock knock.
Who's there?
The interrupting cow.
The interrupting cow wh—
MOOOOOOOOOO!

Knock knock.
Who's there?
Police.
Police who?
Police let us in. It's freezing out here!

What's black and white and noisy?
A zebra with a drum kit.

❖

What's black and white and red all over?
A newspaper.

Knock knock.
Who's there?
Arthur.
Arthur who?
Arthur any biscuits left?

❖

Knock knock.
Who's there?
Scott.
Scott who?
Scott to be me, of course. Were you expecting someone else?

❖

What's black and white and black and white and green?
Two zebras fighting over a pickled gherkin.

❖

What's grey, yellow, white, grey, yellow, white and grey?
An elephant rolling down the hill with a daisy in its mouth.

❖

What's red and black and red and black?
A zebra with sunburn.

Knock knock.
Who's there?
Snow.
Snow who?
Snow business like show business.

❖

Knock knock.
Who's there?
Doughnut.
Doughnut who?
Doughnut open until your birthday!

❖

What's black and white and eats like a horse?
A zebra.

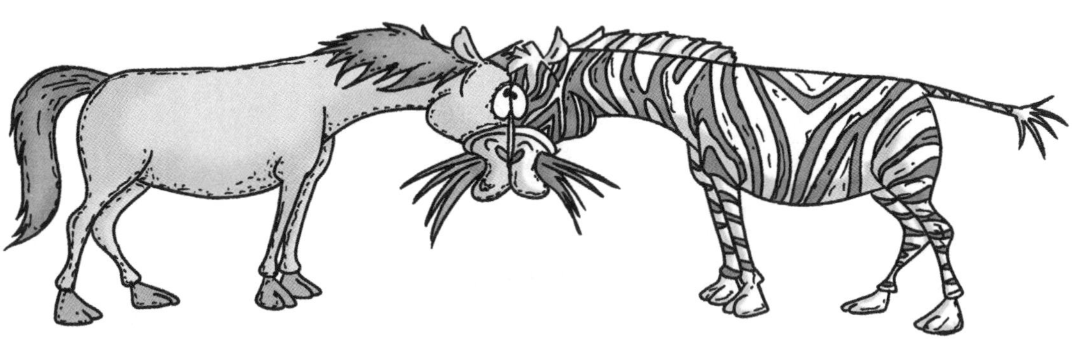

What do you call a man with a car on his head?

Jack.

Knock knock.
Who's there?
Doris.
Doris who?
Doris locked. That's why I had to knock!

❖

Knock knock.
Who's there?
Tank.
Tank who?
You're welcome!

Knock knock.
Who's there?
Boo.
Boo who?
Don't cry. It's only a joke.

❖

Knock knock.
Who's there?
Hawaii.
Hawaii who?
I'm fine, thanks. How are you?

❖

Knock knock.
Who's there?
Archie.
Archie who?
Bless you!

❖

Knock knock.
Who's there?
Ya.
Ya who?
What are you getting so excited about?

Why did the orange stop in the middle of the road?
Because he ran out of juice.

❖

Knock knock.
Who's there?
Nicholas.
Nicholas who?
Nicholas girls get cold in winter.

❖

Knock knock.
Who's there?
Dunnup.
Dunnup who?
Tee hee hee!

❖

Knock knock.
Who's there?
Little old lady.
Little old lady who?
I didn't know you could yodel!

What do you call a man with a seagull on his head?

Cliff.

Knock knock.

Who's there?

A lass.

A lass who?

Isn't that what cowboys use?

❖

How can you tell if there's an elephant in the fridge?

The door won't shut.

❖

What do you call a man with a spade in his head?

Doug.

Why is tap dancing dangerous?
If you slip, you might fall in the sink.

❖

What do you call a man without a spade in his head?
Douglas.

❖

Knock knock.
Who's there?
Ammonia.
Ammonia who?
Ammonia person collecting for charity!

❖

What do you call an overeducated plumber?
A drain surgeon.

What do you call a man with turf on his head?

Pete.

❖

Knock knock.
Who's there?
Wanda.
Wanda who?
Wanda wish you a happy birthday!

❖

What do you call a woman who catches lots of fish in one go?

Annette.

❖

How many crime writers does it take to change a lightbulb?

Two. One to screw it in and the other to give it a good twist at the end.

❖

Knock, knock.
Who's there?
Dishes.
Dishes who?
Dishes a terrible joke!

Knock knock.
Who's there?
Doctor.
Doctor Who?
How did you know it was me?

❖

What do you call a deer with no eyes?
No idea.

❖

What do you call a deer with no eyes who's totally motionless?
Still no idea.

❖

What do you call a deer with no eyes who's totally motionless and is on fire?
Still flaming no idea.

❖

What do you call a man with a toilet on his head?
Lou.

❖

What do you call a lady with two toilets on her head?
Lulu.

Did you hear about the string section of the orchestra that held up the bank?
It was robbery with violins.

❖

Did you hear about the woman who got the job as the human cannonball?
She was fired.

Knock knock.
Who's there?
Theresa.
Theresa who?
Theresa green in summer.

What did one angel say to the other angel?
Halo there!

What do you call a man with his pockets stuffed full of paper bags?
Russell.

❖

What do you call a man with rabbits in his trousers?
Warren.

❖

What begins with "e" and ends with "e" and has a letter in the middle?
An envelope.

What do you call a woman with a frog on her head?
Lily.

❖

What do you call a camel with three humps?
Humphrey.

❖

When is a door not a door?
When it's ajar.

❖

What's green and goes camping?
A Brussels scout.

❖

Why do elephants paint their toenails red?
So they can hide in strawberry patches.

❖

What do you call a man who can't stand up?
Neil.

What should you feed an elf who wants to be taller?
Elf-raising flour.

❖

On which side of the house did Jack's beanstalk grow?
The outside.

❖

What is an archaeologist?
Someone whose career is in ruins.

❖

Did you hear about the accountant with constipation?
He worked it out with a pencil.

❖

What do you call a man who floats on the sea?
Bob.

❖

What was the insect's favourite sport?
Cricket.

Why did the jewel thief have a nice, foamy bubble bath before robbing a rich woman?
He wanted to make a clean getaway.

Did you hear about the dizzy charity worker?
She spent all week doing good turns.

❖

Did you hear about the jewel thief who opened a shop?
He used a crowbar.

❖

Did you hear about the man who went to sleep under the leaky, old car?
He wanted to wake up oily in the morning.

Did you hear about the prisoner who talked v-e-r-y slowly?
It took him 15 years to finish his sentence.

❖

Who can shave six times a day and still have a beard?
A barber.

❖

Why are management meetings always so horribly dull?
They're held in the Bored Room.

❖

What do you call a sheep with no legs?
A cloud.

Did you hear about the tax dodger who got into hot water?
The cold tap was broken.

❖

What do you call a tree with a croaky voice?
A hoarse chestnut.

❖

What do you call a giraffe with one leg?
Eileen.

❖

Have you heard the joke about the bed?
Sorry, it hasn't been made up yet.

❖

Where do pianists go on holiday?
The Florida Keys.

❖

How do you keep a total idiot in suspense?
I'll tell you later.

What do you call a really tiny woman?
Dot.

❖

What did the firefighter's wife get for Christmas?
A ladder in her stocking.

❖

Why did the girl throw the clock out of the window?
She wanted to see time fly.

❖

What do you get if you drop a grand piano down a lift shaft?
A flat miner.

❖

What did the highwayman say to the tap-dancing postman?
Stand and deliver.

❖

How do you know when a filthy robber has taken a bath?
When it goes missing from your bathroom.

What do you get when you cross a dog with an elephant?
A really nervous postman.

❖

What type of dog can tell the time?
A watchdog.

What happened to the clock that fell into the sheep medicine?
It lost all its ticks.

❖

What did one lift say to the other lift?
I think I'm coming down with something.

If you found money in every pocket of your trousers, what would you have?
Someone else's trousers.

What's huge, grey and babbles incoherently when it speaks?
A mumbo jumbo.

❖

Why wouldn't the bald man lend anyone his comb?
He just couldn't part with it.

❖

How do you make your own antifreeze?
Send her to the Antarctic.

How does a policeman listen to music on the beat?
On his iPlod.

❖

How does Jack Frost travel?
By icicle.

❖

Why did the man bash the giggling fortune teller?
He was striking a happy medium.

❖

What did the scarf say to the hat?
You go on ahead and I'll just hang around.

❖

Why did Tinkerbell fly backwards
and forwards between Dover and Calais?
She was a cross-channel fairy.

❖

What's hairy and sneezes?
A coconut with a cold.

Why did the code-breaker spend so long in the percussion section of the orchestra?
He was looking for cymbals.

❖

Why didn't the banana snore?
He didn't want to wake up the rest of the bunch!

❖

Doctor, doctor, I feel like a python.
You can't get round me just like that!

❖

Doctor, doctor, I think I'm a nit.
Just get out of my hair!

❖

Knock knock.
Who's there?
Norma Lee.
Norma Lee who?
Norma Lee I'd ring the doorbell.

Knock knock.
Who's there?
Halle.
Halle who?
Hallelujah!
I'm here to sing Christmas carols!

❖

Doctor, doctor, I think I'm a caterpillar.
Don't worry. You'll soon change.

What do you call a woman who takes people to court?

Sue.

❖

Doctor, doctor, I feel like a mosquito.

Buzz off!

❖

What do you get if you cross a painter with a police officer?

A brush with the law.

Knock knock.
Who's there?
Anna.
Anna who?
Anna one, anna two ...

❖

How many police officers does it take to screw in a lightbulb?
None. It turns itself in.

❖

Why was the clock feeling sick?
It was run down.

❖

Why did the comedy boxer pause?
He was waiting for the punchline.

❖

Knock knock.
Who's there?
Toodle.
Toodle who?
You're going already?

Why did the cockerel cross the road?
To prove that he wasn't a chicken!

❖

Doctor, doctor, I've got flat feet.
Here's a bicycle pump to blow them up again.

❖

Doctor, doctor, I think I'm a cow.
Pull the udder one.

❖

Doctor, doctor, I'm sorry I'm late for my appointment, but I sprained my ankle.
That's a lame excuse!

❖

Knock knock.
Who's there?
Eve.
Eve who?
Eve-ning!

What do you call a woman who sets fire to all her bills?

Bernadette.

❖

Doctor, doctor, I just swallowed a sheep!

How do you feel?

Baaaaaaaaad.

❖

Doctor, doctor, I've lost my memory!

When did this happen?

When did what happen?

A Shaggy Dog...

Goldilocks was taking a stroll one lovely, sunny afternoon when she came across a charming house hidden in the middle of the woods. A warm, inviting cooking smell was wafting out of the open door. Suddenly Goldilocks felt really hungry! So she crept in, her nose following the sweet smell. There were three bowls of porridge on the table. "Hello? Anyone home?" she called out, but no one answered.

Her tummy rumbled noisily, so Goldilocks sat down at the table and took a mouthful from the first bowl. "Ouch!" she exclaimed, it was too hot, so she tried the second bowl. "Yuk!" she cried, it was too cold, so she tried the third bowl. "Mmm…" This porridge was just right.

Yummy, sweet and delicious. Goldilocks gulped down the whole lot and licked the bowl clean. After that she felt really, really tired. Letting out a big yawn, she got up and searched for a bed so she could have a nap. She looked in all the rooms on the bottom floor, but found nothing, so she went up the stairs, feeling really sleepy.

She went into the first room, "At last!" she said, as she dived onto the big bed. "Ow!" shouted Goldilocks, the bed was too hard, so she went into the second room where she found another bed, which she hopped into. "Oh, no," said sleepy Goldilocks, it was much too soft, so dragging her feet, she went into the third room where she immediately screamed in surprise! Inside were three little pigs, all staring at her.

"What are you three doing here?" said Goldilocks, "You're in the wrong fairy tale!"

"No we're not," answered one of the pigs. "This is a two-story house."

Knock knock.

Who's there?

Eva.

Eva who?

Eva fancied double glazing?

❖

How many amoebas does it take to change a lightbulb?

One. No, two! No, four! No, eight ... sixteen ... thirty-two!

❖

Why did the Roman chicken cross the road?

She was worried that someone would Caesar.

Knock knock.
Who's there?
Maia.
Maia who?
Maia totally pooped marathon-runner have a sit down, please?

❖

Doctor, doctor, I can't stop pulling funny faces.
What's wrong with that?
The people with funny faces are getting fed up with me.

❖

What gets wetter the more it dries?
A towel.

❖

Did you hear about the magical tractor?
It turned into a field.

❖

What do you call a man with sports equipment on his head?
Jim.

Doctor, doctor, I feel flushed.
You must have flu.
No, I walked here.

❖

Doctor, doctor, can you give me something for my kidneys?
Yes, here's half a pound of steak.

❖

Where did the police officer live?
999 Letsby Avenue.

❖

Knock knock.
Who's there?
Scott.
Scott who?
Scott nothing to do with you.

❖

Doctor, doctor, you've removed my tonsils,
my adenoids and my appendix, but I still feel ill.
That's quite enough out of you.

Knock knock.
Who's there?
Twit too.
Twit too who?
That's a fantastic owl impression!

Doctor, doctor, I have asparagus sprouting from my ears.
How did that happen?
I've no idea. I planted beetroot.

❖

What type of degree was the sheep awarded?
The BA.

Doctor, doctor, I think I'm a frog.
So what's the problem?
I'm sure I'm going to croak.

❖

Why didn't the skeleton cross the road?
He didn't have the guts.

❖

Doctor, doctor, my throat is very sore.
Open that window and stick your tongue out.
Will that make me feel better?
No. I can't stand my next-door neighbour.

Knock knock.
Who's there?
Lydia.
Lydia who?
Lydia teapot looks a bit loose. Shall I fix it?

❖

Doctor, doctor, I keep thinking I'm Mozart.
I'll be with you in a minuet.

❖

Doctor, doctor, I'm not very tall.
You'll just have to be a little patient.

❖

What do you call a man with a car number plate on the back of his head?
Reg.

❖

Why do ducks eat biscuits?
Because they're quackers!

What do you call a man who pickles himself in salty water?
Brian.

❖

Doctor, doctor, I've got an urge to hang dangerously from the window ledge!
Hold on a minute.

❖

Knock knock.
Who's there?
Hugh.
Hugh who?
Hugh d'you think it is!

❖

Doctor, doctor, I'm allergic to the high jump.
Don't worry, you'll soon get over it!

❖

Doctor, doctor, I'm addicted to fishing.
When you're feeling better, drop me a line.

Who delivers presents to dogs on Christmas Eve?
Santa Paws.

❖

What do you call a man who squeezes through your letterbox?
Bill.

❖

What's the funniest cuppa?
The one you drink at a tee-hee-hee party.

❖

How many magicians does it take to change a lightbulb?
It depends what you'd like to change it into!

Why did the shaggy sheep cross the road?

To get to the baa baa shop.

Man One: My wife's gone on holiday.

Man Two: Jamaica?

Man One: No, she went of her own accord.

❖

Doctor, doctor, I feel like a bowl of custard.

Sit down and don't be so thick.

❖

Man Two: My wife's gone on holiday too.

Man One: Jakarta?

Man Two: No, she flew.

Knock knock.
Who's there?
Claudette.
Claudette who?
Claudette all of my chocolate!

❖

Doctor, doctor, I feel like a cup of tea.
So do I. Make me one while you're at it.

❖

How many aerospace engineers does it change to change a lightbulb?
None. It's not rocket science!

❖

What do you call a man who's good at fixing things?
Andy.

❖

What were the pirate's two favourite letters?
Oooooh and arrrghhhh

What do you call a woman who likes to help old people with their shopping?
Carrie.

❖

Doctor, doctor, I keep thinking I'm a chicken.
Get stuffed!

❖

Knock knock.
Who's there?
Justin.
Justin who?
Justin time for dinner!

❖

What do you call a man who wins every race he enters?
Victor.

❖

Why did the elastic chicken cross the road?
She wanted to stretch her legs.

Doctor, doctor, I feel like a snooker player.

You're going to pot.

❖

Constantinople is a very long word. Can you spell it?

C, O, N, S, T, A, N, T, I, N, O, P, L, E.

Don't be silly! It is spelt like this … I, T!

❖

Doctor, doctor, my eyesight's getting worse.

I'll say it is. This is the library.

What do you call a woman with a nut tree on her head?

Hazel.

❖

What do you call a man who can't help pinching things?

Nick.

What do you call a woman with a cat on her head?

Kitty.

❖

What do you call a woman who sits in a little dish?

Olive.

Doctor, doctor, I think I'm a bungee jumper!
You've probably been a bit up and down lately.

❖

Doctor, doctor, my legs feel like jelly.
Don't worry. They'll be better in a trifle.

❖

What did one wall say to the other wall?
I'll meet you at the corner.

❖

What do you call a woman who does impressions of emergency vehicles?
Nina.

❖

Knock knock.
Who's there?
Isobel.
Isobel who?
Isobel really necessary when you have such a great door knocker?

What do you call a man with a road map on his head?
Miles.

❖

Did you hear about the woman with the big fluffy hat called Cynthia?
That's a funny name for a hat.

❖

What do you call a man with three raincoats?
Max.

❖

How did the chicken get to the other side without being squashed?
It was clucky.

❖

One.
How many fortune tellers does it take to change a lightbulb?

Doctor, doctor, I just swallowed plutonium!
Hmm. You may get atomic ache.

❖

What do you call a man with an oversized raincoat?
Big Mac.

Doctor, doctor, I keep thinking I'm an alarm clock.
I'll see you in a tick.

Why did the pig cross the road really, really slowly?

Because it was a road hog.

❖

Why did the chewing gum cross the road?

Because it was stuck to the chicken's foot.

How do you get an idiot to laugh at the end of the day?

Tell him a joke at the start of the day.

❖

Doctor, doctor, I keep thinking I'm a stand-up comedian.

You must be joking.

Knock knock.
Who's there?
Anya.
Anya who?
Anya best behaviour, please!

❖

What do you get if you cross a honeydew and a sheepdog?
A melon collie.

❖

How many librarians does it take to change a lightbulb?
Two. One to screw it in and one to say, "Shhhhhhh!" at the squeaking noise.

❖

Knock knock.
Who's there?
Barbara.
Barbara who?
Barbara black sheep, have you any wool?

What do you get if you dip convicts into quick-drying cement?

Hardened criminals.

❖

What do you call a man with a huge truck on his head?

Laurie.

❖

What did one lightbulb say to the other lightbulb?

I'm going out tonight.

❖

What has one foot and four legs?

A bed.

❖

Why did the chicken cross the football pitch?

Because the referee whistled for a fowl.

❖

Knock knock.
Who's there?
Candy.
Candy who?
Candy cow jump over the moon?

Seaside Sniggers

A man walks into a fish and chip shop and says,
"Got any cod left?"
"Yes," replies the owner.
"Shouldn't have made so many then, should you?"

❖

How did pirates sleep on galleons?
With their eyes shut.

❖

There are two goldfish in a tank. What does one goldfish say to the other goldfish?
"Do you know how to drive this thing?"

❖

What did the sea say to the dolphin?
Nothing, it just waved.

❖

What do you call a fish with no eyes?
Fsh.

What do you call a fish with four eyes?
Fiiiish.

❖

What do you call a pirate with a wooden leg, a very pointy hook and a parrot stuck in each ear?
Anything you like, he can't hear you!

❖

How much did the pirate pay for his wooden leg and terrifyingly sharp hook?
An arm and a leg.

❖

How do cod and mackerel watch the news?
On a telefishon.

How did the tiny shellfish cross the seabed?

By taxi crab.

Why couldn't the pirate play cards?

Because he was sitting on the deck.

❖

What's yellow and dangerous?

Shark-infested custard.

❖

What's black, incredibly rude and floats on water?

Crude oil.

What lives under the sea and carries lots of people to and fro?
An octo-bus.

❖

Why do fish avoid computers?
They don't want to get caught in the internet.

❖

Why are pirates called pirates?
Because they ARRRRRR!

❖

What happened when the boat carrying blue paint hit the boat carrying red paint?
All of the passengers were marooned.

❖

Why did the animal welfare officer close down the fish and chip shop?
They were battering the fish.

❖

What do you find in the middle of the ocean?
The letter "e".

Why did the sailor carry a piece of rope on to the boat?

Because he was the skipper.

❖

What's a pirate's favourite boxing punch?

The right hook.

❖

What's a pirate's favourite fairy tale?

Booty and the Beast.

❖

What's a pirate's favourite letter of the alphabet?

R.

❖

Why did the pirate's phone go, "beeeep … beeeep … beeeep?"

He left it off the hook.

❖

Why didn't the sea captain's radio work in rough seas?

It was on the wrong wavelength.

What do you get if you cross a snowman and a shark?

Frostbite.

❖

What's the best way to get in touch with a fish?

Drop it a line.

❖

What's the difference between a fish and a piano?

You can't tuna fish.

❖

Which is the most precious fish in the world?

A goldfish.

What did the jazz musician eat for his fish supper?
He had sole.

❖

What type of lettuce did they serve on the Titanic?
Iceberg.

❖

Where do very young fish go every morning?
Plaice school.

❖

What are the strongest creatures in the ocean?
Mussels.

What did the blue whale say when he collided with the bottlenose dolphin?

"I didn't do it on porpoise."

❖

How did the magician cut the sea in half?

With a sea saw.

❖

What's the laziest fish in the world?

The kipper.

❖

Which is the saddest creature in the sea?

The blue whale.

❖

What is a fish's favourite party game?

Tide-and-seek.

❖

Which seabird can dance?

A pelican-can.

What does a fish supper taste like?
Brill.

❖

What does an octopus wear in the winter?
A coat of arms.

❖

What do the ocean and a Christmas pudding have in common?
They're both full of currents!

❖

Who was the first underwater spy?
James Pond.

What happens when you throw a purple rock into the Red Sea?

It gets wet.

❖

What's green and knobbly and spends a lot of time under the sea?

An avocado wearing scuba gear.

❖

Where do you weigh a whale?

At a whale-weigh station.

❖

What's the best way to catch a fish?

Get someone to throw it at you.

❖

Which is the shiniest fish in the sea?

The starfish.

❖

What is a sailor's favourite colour?

Navy blue.

Who lives in a sandcastle?
A sandwitch.

❖

What's a carpenter's favourite sea creature?
A hammerhead shark.

❖

What do you get if you cross a fish with an elephant?
Swimming trunks.

❖

Who do fish borrow money from?
A loan shark.

❖

What do you find on very small beaches?
Microwaves.

❖

Why are seagulls called seagulls?
Because if they flew over bays, they would be bagels.

Where did the ship go when it was feeling poorly?

It visited the docks.

Why was the pupil's school report wet?

Because her grades were all below C level.

❖

Why are dolphins cleverer than humans?

They can train a human to stand at the side of a pool and throw fish to them.

❖

How does a pod of dolphins make its mind up?

They flipper coin.

What does a bridegroom wear to an underwater wedding?

A very wet suit.

Why don't you ever see penguins near the UK?

They're scared of Wales.

❖

Why can't penguins fly?

They can't afford aeroplane tickets.

❖

What did the seaweed say when it was stuck to the bottom of the speedboat?

"Kelp!!!!!"

What do penguins have for lunch?
Icebergers.

❖

Which sea creatures are the biggest cry babies?
Whales.

❖

Why wasn't the girl scared when a shark swam past her?
It was a man-eating shark.

❖

What do you call a man-eating cod?
Fish-ious.

❖

What is an eel's favourite party dance?
The conger.

❖

What do you give a deaf fish?
A herring aid.

Why did the Victorian holidaymaker float?
His trunks were made of wood.

❖

What did the seaweed say when it got stuck in the rock pool?
Kelp! Kelp!

❖

What do you call a girl who stands in the sea and lets people walk all over her?
Pia.

❖

When's the best time to dive into a swimming pool?
When there's water in it.

❖

Why did the holidaymakers smell of salt and pepper?
They were seasoned travellers.

❖

What dries as it gets wetter?
A towel.

What did the dancer with two left feet wear to the holiday disco?

Flip-flips.

What's the sweetest type of music you get beside the seaside?

Rock.

❖

What did the wave say to the sea?

It's high tide I got out of here.

Did you hear about the stick of rock that was hard of hearing?
It was stone deaf.

❖

What do pickpockets do when they spot the
police at the funfair?
Dodgem.

❖

What do you call an ice cream man with a 99 in one ear
and an ice lolly in the other?
Anything you like, he can't hear you.

What do you call a man-made Greek holiday island?
Con-Crete.

❖

What was the hairdresser's favourite funfair ride?
The roller coaster.

❖

What was the ballroom dancer's favourite funfair ride?
The waltzer.

❖

What did the Scuba diver say to the ship?
I can see your bottom.

❖

What did one ice cream seller say to the other ice cream seller?
Have an ice day!

❖

Why did the crab blush?
Because the seaweed.

Why did the fish take such a long time to make his mind up?
He wanted to mullet over.

❖

What are qualified divers presented with?
A deep-loma.

❖

What kind of hairstyle does the sea have?
Wavy.

❖

What is a pirate's favourite school subject?
Arrrrrrt.

Silly Sport

What do you call a pig that does karate?

A pork chop.

Why wouldn't the football player cross the road?

It was offside.

❖

How do Formula One witches travel?

By vroomstick.

❖

Which part of a rugby stadium never stays the same?

The changing rooms.

What's striped, furry and goes "meeeeeowwwwwwww"?
A cat in a racing car.

❖

Why is it sweltering hot after a football match?
All the fans have gone home.

❖

Did you hear about the sports equipment manufacturer with his stereo on full blast?
He was making a racket.

❖

What did Robin Hood say when he was almost hit at the archery tournament?
"That was an arrow escape!"

❖

Did you hear about the Formula One car with a wooden engine?
It wooden go.

What should a football team do if the pitch is flooded?
Bring on their subs.

❖

Which part of a football pitch smells the nicest?
The scenter spot.

❖

What do martial artists suffer from in the winter?
Kung-flu.

❖

What do you get if you cross a bunch of crazy jokers with a football team?
Mad Jester United.

❖

What do you get if you cross a football team with a tub of ice cream?
Aston Vanilla.

Why wouldn't the skeleton bungee jump into the Grand Canyon?

He had no guts.

What's the fastest milk in the world?

Full-fat milk. It's pasteurised before you know it.

❖

What's the fastest vegetable on earth?

A runner bean.

❖

Why are goalkeepers stinking rich?

Because they are good savers.

What's green and runs around the garden?

A hedge.

❖

What did the parachuting insect shout as it jumped out of the aeroplane?

"Earwig go!"

❖

Why was Cinderella a terrible football player?

Because she played with one glass slipper on.

Which animal is always found at cricket matches?

A bat.

❖

Did you hear about the scarecrow who won a gold medal?

He was out standing in his field.

❖

Which way does a chicken swim round a pool?

Cluck-wise.

❖

What did the golfer eat for lunch?

A sand wedge.

❖

What do a top striker and a magician have in common?

They both do hat tricks.

❖

How did the football pitch turn into a right-angled triangle?

Somebody took a corner.

What do babies and football players have in common?
They're both really good at dribbling.

❖

Where do footballers go dancing?
At a football.

❖

If there's a referee in football, what is there in bowls?
Soup!

❖

Which insect was terrible in goal?
The fumblebee.

❖

What is a marathon runner's favourite subject?
Jography.

❖

Did you hear about the rugby-mad monster with nine heads?
He had nine caps.

Who can spot promising players and tie seventeen
different types of knot?
A scout.

❖

Why did the football player kick the ball around
his own back garden?
It was a home game.

❖

Why did the basketball players spin the ball on their fingertips?
Because it was the Whirled Cup.

❖

What's a horse's favourite sport?
Stable tennis.

What kind of cats are great at bowling?

Alley cats.

What happened to the football player
who wore perfume?

He was scent off.

❖

What do you call a fishy goal?

The Hand of Cod.

❖

Why did the ambulance arrive on the football pitch
after 90 minutes were up?

The players were into injury time.

Do undersea creatures play football?
Yes, they do. There are 20,000 Leagues Under the Sea.

❖

Why is it easy to forecast the weather on match days?
There are always showers after the final whistle.

❖

Why was the pirate such an amazing boxer?
Because of his left hook.

❖

Did you hear about the sticky,
see-through football player?
He was a transfer.

❖

If marathon runners suffer from athlete's foot,
what do soldiers suffer from?
Missile toe.

Why was the tennis court wet?
Because of the floodlights.

❖

Did you hear about the crowd of potatoes watching the match?
They kept their eyes peeled.

❖

In which league do French fries play football?
In the Premierchip.

❖

What happened when the monkey scored a goal?
The crowd went bananas.

❖

Why didn't the dog do martial arts?
Because it was a boxer.

❖

Why do football players stay cool during a match?
Because of the fans.

How did the goalkeeper send his birthday cards?

By goalpost.

❖

What do footballers drink?

Penal-tea.

❖

What should you give a golfer as a wedding gift?

A teepot.

❖

Why is it dangerous to tell jokes while ice skating?

The ice might crack up.

Why did the golfer wear two pairs of trousers?

In case he got a hole in one.

Where do old bowling balls get thrown?

In the gutter.

❖

What's the angriest part of a goal?

The crossbar.

❖

What's the hungriest part of a goal?

The goalmouth.

What do you call a really tiny sports' fan?

A speck-tator.

❖

What's a footballer's favourite pudding?

Pitch melba.

❖

Did you hear about the monk
who longed to be a football player?

He was trying to kick the habit.

❖

Why did the football player hesitate at the traffic lights?

He was a dreadful crosser.

❖

When does it rain football players?

When it's teaming down.

What did the cricket glove say to the cricket ball?
"Catch you later!"

❖

Why was the computer such a terrific golfer?
It had a hard drive.

❖

How do you start a teddy bear race?
"Ready, teddy, go!"

❖

What do a blindfolded midfielder and a car with no steering wheel have in common?
They are both really dreadful at taking corners.

What did the crowd shout
when the ghost flew into the net?
Ghoul!

❖

Why do basketball players love biscuits?
They can dunk them.

❖

What's the best time of the year
to bounce on a trampoline?
Springtime!

❖

Why did the runner never forget anything?
He was always jogging his memory.

❖

How do you start a jelly race?
Get set!

Did you hear about the martial-arts specialist with a bad cold?
It was kung flu.

❖

If two collars raced each other, how would it all end?
In a tie.

❖

When do you need a wombat?
When you're playing a game of wom.

❖

Did you hear about the bonkers golfer?
He was a crack putt.

❖

What does a table-tennis table smell like?
It has a terrible ping-pong.

❖

What do martial arts experts cook on the barbeque?
Karate chops.

What do you say to a pole vaulter?
Hiya!

❖

Why did the cricket captain hire a new chef?
He needed a good batter.

❖

Why was Cinderella so terrible at tennis?
She had a pumpkin for a coach.

What's green and hard?
A frog in boxing gloves.

What goes putt-putt-putt-putt-putt?
A dreadful golfer.

❖

If you get an umpire in cricket and a referee in football, what do you get in bowls?
Fruit.

Why was Cinderella no good at football?
She kept running away from the ball.

❖

What can you serve, but never eat?
A tennis ball.

❖

Why couldn't the car play football?
Because it only had one boot.

❖

How many windy gymnasts does it take to stink out a gymnasium?
A phew.

❖

Why did the target run away just before the archery contest began?
It wanted to make an arrow escape.

Why did the football player use special face wash?
Because of his penalty spot.

❖

What's the fastest cake in the world?
Scone.

❖

How do you know when a referee is having a smashing time?
He whistles while he works.

❖

Why was Tarzan banned from the golf course?
He screamed with every swing.

❖

Did you hear about the football player who's ambition was to be an artist?
He liked to draw.

Funny Food

What happened to the hyena who accidentally swallowed an OXO cube?
He became a laughing stock.

❖

Why didn't the boy with a sausage up his nose and a chocolate bar in his ear feel well?
He wasn't eating properly.

❖

What's worse than biting into an apple and finding a worm?
Finding half a worm.

How do Welsh people eat cheese?

Caerphilly.

❖

Why is an old-fashioned radio like roasted pork?

They both have lots of crackling.

❖

Have you heard the joke about the butter?

Sorry, I can't tell you because you might spread it.

❖

How do you make a chicken stew?

Keep it waiting for a couple of hours.

❖

What happens if you eat Christmas decorations?

You get tinselitis.

❖

What's the best day of the week to eat ice cream?

Sundae!

How do you make a Mexican chilli?
Send him to Siberia.

❖

How do you make a sausage roll?
Push it down a hill.

❖

What sort of jokes would a man who likes Cheddar tell?
Really cheesy ones.

❖

What's orange and points North?
A magnetic carrot.

❖

What did the egg in the monastery say?
"Out of the frying pan, into the friar!"

❖

What did the banana say to the grape?
Nothing. Bananas can't talk.

What do snowmen eat for breakfast?

Snowflakes.

What colour is a burp?

Burple.

❖

How do you make a glass of milkshake?

Give it a fright.

❖

Why did the jelly wobble?

Because it saw the milk shake.

How did the banana know he was ill?

He wasn't peeling well.

What did the waiter say when the horse walked into the café?

"Why the long face?"

❖

What do you call an aeroplane passenger covered in salt and pepper?

A seasoned traveller.

❖

What did the baby corn say to the mama corn?

Where's the pop corn?

What do you call a piece of fruit wearing a gag?
Peachless.

❖

What do you get if you cross a comedian and an orange?
Peels of laughter.

❖

What do you get if you cross a biscuit and a steamroller?
Crumbs.

❖

What happened to the rhubarb thief?
He ended up in custody.

❖

Why did the ant run across the top of the cereal packet?
Because it said, "tear along the dotted line".

❖

What is small, round and can't help laughing?
A tickled onion.

What's the best thing to put in an apple pie?

A spoon.

❖

What did one plate say to the other plate?

Lunch is on me.

❖

What's small, green, round and goes up, down, up, down?

A pea in a lift.

❖

What's yellow and stupid?

Thick custard.

❖

Did you hear about the egg that was tickled far too much?

It cracked up.

❖

How do you turn light chocolate into dark chocolate?

Turn the light off.

What do you call a worried turnip?
An edgy veggie.

❖

What do you give a dog with a temperature?
Fried onions, mustard and ketchup. They're the best things for a hot dog.

❖

How do you make a fruit punch?
Give it boxing lessons.

Which part of the sponge cake did the dentist like best?
The filling.

❖

What do you get if you whisk butter, sugar and eggs together for 37 minutes exactly?
A sore arm.

❖

What's green, hairy and goes up, down, up, down?
A gooseberry on a trampoline.

Why did the management consultant spit food at his client?
He was giving feedback.

❖

Why did the rhubarb go out with a prune?
Because he couldn't find a date.

❖

Why did the tomato go red?
Because it saw the salad dressing.

❖

Why is a Brussels sprout small and green?
Because if it was big and red it would be a fire engine.

❖

Why was the stale biscuit so sad?
He was feeling crummy.

❖

What does a greengrocer who is six feet tall weigh?
Vegetables.

Why couldn't the poppy seed leave the bowling alley?
Because he was on a roll.

❖

Why did the schoolboy eat his homework?
The teacher told him it was a piece of cake.

❖

What do you get if you put five ducks in a box?
A box of quackers.

❖

What's a cannibal's favourite takeaway?
Pizza with everyone on it.

❖

Why did the man eat at the investment bank?
He loved rich food.

❖

Where do people swap jugs of gravy with each other?
At the Stock Exchange.

What did the teddy bear say when he was offered second helpings?

No, thanks. I'm stuffed!

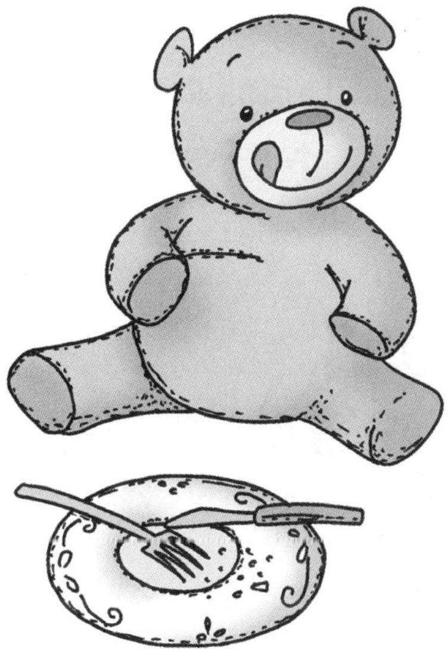

Did you hear about the fruit salad without any pink fruit in it?

It was peachless.

❖

Where do monkeys sleep?

In ape-ricots.

❖

Which musical instrument goes really well with cheese?

The pickle-o.

What has lots of ears, but can't hear anything at all?
A cornfield.

❖

What's green and sings in the vegetable patch?
Elvis Parsley.

How do you make a cheese puff?
Chase it round the kitchen.

❖

Why did the chef serve frozen steak?
He wanted it to melt in the mouth.

What did the flamenco-dancing farmer say to his chickens?
"Oh, lay!"

❖

Where do fish keep their savings?
In riverbanks.

❖

What kind of fruit do terribly posh people love to eat?
Toff-ee apples.

❖

What's round, delicious and very, very slippery?
An oiled sweet.

❖

What's round, shiny and says, "ahem"?
A cough sweet.

❖

Who solved the sweet-shop mystery?
Sherbert Holmes.

What do red squirrels eat?

Gingernuts.

❖

Did you hear about the chocolate-coated train?

It was a cocoa-motive.

❖

What did the classical musician love to eat?

Organ-ic chocolate.

❖

What type of cheese is made backwards?

Edam.

❖

How do you make hot chocolate?

Leave it out in the sun.

❖

What's the best thing to put in a chocolate bar?

Your teeth.

Did you hear about the elf who ate too fast?

He was goblin his food.

Why did robbers raid the sweet shop?

They wanted the lolly.

❖

When's the best time of day to eat a crisp apple?

Crunchtime.

❖

How many decorations should you put on top of fairy cakes?

Hundreds and thousands.

What is the highest pudding in Paris?

The Trifle Tower.

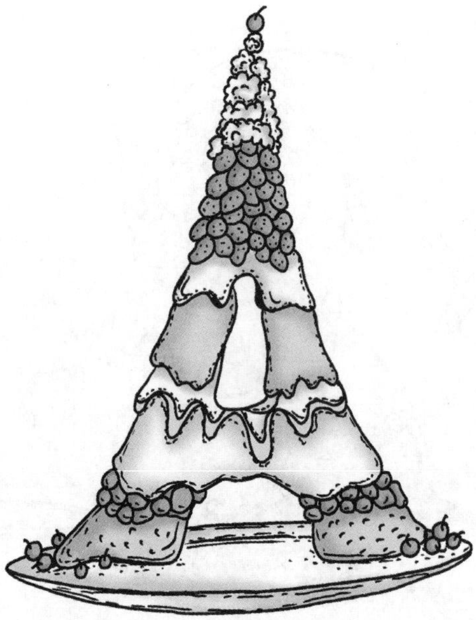

What did the sherbert say to the humbug?

"Hi, sweetie!"

❖

Which planet has a fruity centre and is covered in icing?

Mars-ipan.

❖

Why did the cream squeal?

Someone was whipping it.

What do elves make sandwiches with?
Shortbread.

❖

Why did the biscuit cry?
Because his mum had been a wafer so long.

❖

What noise does a nut make when it sneezes?
"Cashew!"

❖

What kind of room can you eat?
A mushroom.

❖

Which fruit never ever gets lonely?
A pear.

❖

What did the Hungarian ghost eat for dinner?
Ghoulash.

❖

Why did the bacon laugh?
Because the egg cracked a yolk.

A Shaggy Dog...

Once there was a pair of young weevils. The little insects were the best of friends and did everything together – they played together, nibbled the local farmer's crops together and laughed at each other's silly jokes (which were very silly indeed).

But as the weevils grew up, they went their separate ways. One weevil became a champion eater. He gobbled everything that the local farmer grew, munching his way through meadow after meadow of delicious crops. And when he'd finished, he moved on to the next farm and the one after that.

The bigger he became, the more he ate. In the world of weevils, he became very famous indeed. In fact, he was a celebrity weevil.

The other weevil was more of a picky eater. He looked for the tastiest ears of corn and rejected the rest, so he never grew big or famous. And he definitely wasn't a celebrity.

One day, a weevil TV crew decided to make a documentary of the celebrity weevil's life story. They came to interview the unknown weevil and asked all about his old friend. "That's interesting," said the weevil interviewer when they'd heard all about the celebrity weevil's early years.

"I have just one last question. Why is it that you never hit the big time? You've never destroyed an entire crop in your whole life."

"Well," said the insect. "I'm the lesser of two weevils, you see."

What do you get if you cross a Roman emperor with a lettuce and a tomato?
Caesar salad.

❖

When is the best time to eat fresh asparagus?
When you're hungry.

❖

Where do burgers dance?
At meatballs.

❖

Why did the burger refuse to star in a blockbuster movie?
The roll wasn't good enough.

❖

Did you hear about Mr Cole the scientist who sliced cabbage very thinly, added carrot, onion, a sprinkling of raisins and a dollop of mayonnaise?
He invented Cole's Law.

Why did the potato cry?
Its peelings were hurt.

❖

What did one gooseberry say to the other gooseberry?
If you hadn't been so juicy, we wouldn't be in this jam.

❖

What is orange and sounds like a parrot?
A carrot.

❖

Did you hear about the strawberry who attended charm school?
He became a real fruit smoothie.

Why did the orange go to the doctor?
He wasn't peeling too well.

❖

How do you make an apple puff?
Chase it round the park.

❖

Did you hear about the apple crumble, rhubarb crumble and gooseberry crumble trial?
They all ended up in custardy.

Which two meals can you never have for breakfast?
Lunch and dinner.

❖

How do you make golden soup?
With 18 carrots.

❖

What's the difference between roast beef and pea soup?
You can roast beef.

❖

How do you make an onion giggle?
Pickle it!

❖

What's the scariest confectionary of all?
Shockolate

❖

Why did the orange stop rolling down the slope?
It didn't have any juice left.

What kind of scones do pilots prefer?

Plain.

❖

What kind of meal do climbers eat on top of a mountain?

High tea.

❖

A pizza walks into a bar and asks for a roast dinner.

"I'm sorry," says the barman. "We don't serve food."

❖

Why did the carrot look down the toilet?

He wondered where the peas had gone.

❖

What is the one vegetable that you should never ever take on a boat?

A leek.

❖

What do you call an overweight pumpkin?

A plumpkin.

Did you hear about the man who fell over in the Indian restaurant?

He slipped into a korma.

❖

Did you hear about the French chef who was a champion first-aider too?

He gave patients the quiche of life.

❖

Why was the pasta kept in the colander?

There was a restraining order.

❖

Which fruit once ruled the world?

Alexander the Grape.

What do sweet-shop owners use to clean their teeth?

Candyfloss.

What starts with T, ends with T and is full of T?

A teapot.

❖

Why did the man eat yeast and furniture polish for breakfast?

He wanted to rise and shine.

❖

Why was the undercover agent sacked from
his job at the greasy spoon café?

He kept spilling the beans.

Cosmic Capers

How do you get a baby astronaut to go to sleep?

Rocket.

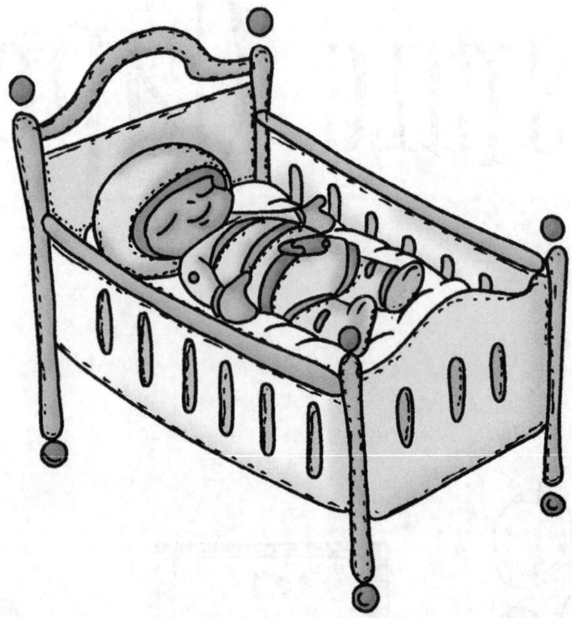

Did you hear about the cashew who went into orbit?

He was an astronut.

❖

What did one asteroid say to the other asteroid?

"Pleased to meteor."

❖

What's ET short for?

Because he has little legs.

Why don't astronauts take eggs into space?
Because eggs're terrestrial!

❖

When do astronauts eat?
At launch time.

❖

Which is the most precious planet?
Saturn. It has a lot of rings.

❖

What do you put on a space horse?
A saddle-lite.

❖

What do young astronauts sit on during take-off?
Booster seats.

If meteorites collide with planets, what do you call meteorites that miss?
Meteowrongs.

❖

What do aliens cook their breakfast on?
An unidentified frying object.

❖

How did the alien tie his shoelaces?
With an astroknot.

❖

What do you call a spaceship with a faulty thermostat?
A frying saucer.

❖

Why don't aliens celebrate each other's birthdays?
They don't like to give away their presents.

Why was the thirsty astronaut loitering near the computer keyboard?
He was looking for the space bar.

❖

Where do you find black holes?
In black socks.

❖

How do you know when the moon isn't hungry?
When it's full.

What type of songs do planets love to hear?
Nep-tunes.

What do spacemen play when they're orbiting Earth?
Astronauts and crosses.

❖

How do you know if the spaceship's engine is running?
When you have to run after it!

❖

What did the Metric alien say to the human?
"Take me to your litre."

What totally bonkers insect lives on the moon?

A lunar-tick.

❖

What kind of poems do you find in outer space?

Uni-verse.

❖

Where does Dr Who buy his sundried tomatoes?

At a dalekatessen.

❖

What type of astronaut can jump higher than a house?

All of them – houses can't jump.

❖

Did you hear about the supersonic egg?

It couldn't be beaten.

What's the centre of gravity?
The letter V.

❖

What sort of turf do aliens play football on?
Astroturf.

❖

What did the alien say to the petrol pump?
"It's very rude to stick your finger in your ear when I'm talking to you!"

❖

Where do aliens go to build sandcastles?
The galax-seaside.

❖

Which star is the most dangerous?
The shooting star.

Did you hear the one about the spaceship from the far-off galaxy?

It was out of this world.

❖

What did the NASA astronaut wear?

Apollo-neck jumper.

❖

Which star wears dark glasses?

A film star.

Why don't astronauts keep their jobs for long?
Because after their training they're always fired.

❖

Why don't astronauts get hungry until they've been in space for a few hours?
They've just had a big launch.

❖

Did you hear about the alien with perfect eyesight?
He had 20-20-20 vision.

Which astronaut wears the biggest space helmet?
The one with the biggest head.

❖

Why didn't the Apollo astronauts stay on the moon?
Because it was full.

❖

What do you get if you cross Earth's atmosphere and a hot drink?
Gravi-tea.

❖

How did the aliens hurt the farmer?
They landed on his corn.

❖

Where do little green men get their eggs?
From the little green hen.

What did Venus say to Saturn?
"Why not give me a ring sometime?"

❖

What is an alien's favourite type of sweet?
A Martian-mallow.

❖

What should a car driver do if he sees a space man?
Park in it, man.

Why did the girl become an astronaut?
Because she was no earthly good.

❖

What do you call an overweight alien?
An extra-cholesterol.

❖

How does the barber cut the man in the moon's hair?
E-clipse it.

❖

Where do martians go to drink?
A Mars Bar.

❖

How do astronomers know that the universe isn't heavy?
Because distances are measured in light years.

Why are parties on the moon always rubbish?

There's no atmosphere.

What did the alien Santa say when he visited Earth?

UFO-O-O.

❖

What does the man in the moon use instead of plates?

Satellite dishes.

❖

What's the easiest way to experience time travel?

Throw your clock at the wall.

Why did the astrophysicist fit a knocker on his front door?
He wanted to win the No Bell Prize.

❖

Why did the alien spacecraft land
outside the bedroom door?
The landing light was on.

❖

What did the alien say to the plant?
"Take me to your weeder."

❖

What happened when the astrophysicist
slammed his front door?
There was a Big Bang.

❖

How many astronomers
does it take to change a lightbulb?
None. They prefer the dark.

If Martians live on Mars and Venutians live on Venus and Saturnians live on Saturn, who lives on Pluto?
Fleas.

❖

Big brother: If this planet is Mars, what's that one?
Little brother: Pa's.

❖

What's the most important thing to do if you're going to have a party in space?
Plan-et.

❖

How does the Solar System hold up its trousers?
With an asteroid belt.

❖

Did you hear about the man who was whisked away by alien teddy bears?
He had a close encounter of the furred kind.

What's big, bright, round and very, very silly?

A fool moon.

❖

What holds the moon up?

Moon beams.

❖

What do you call an alien with five eyes?

Aliiiiien.

What did the boy star say to the girl star?
"Do you want to glow out with me?"

❖

Where do aliens leave their spaceships?
At parking meteors.

❖

What do aliens rest their teacups on?
Flying saucers.

Last Laughs

How do trees get on the internet?

They log in.

What do you get if you cross a sheep with a trampoline?

A woolly jumper.

❖

What's green and smells of yellow paint?

Green paint.

❖

What did the Spanish firefighter call his twin sons?

José and Hose B.

Why would you take a mallet to bed with you?

So you could hit the sack.

❖

What type of house weighs the least of all?

A light house.

❖

What did the traffic light say to the car?

"Don't look, I'm changing!"

❖

What do Rupert The Bear and Winnie The Pooh have in common?

They both have the same middle name.

❖

How do rich people dance?

Cheque to cheque.

❖

How can you walk through walls?

Open the door.

Where do books go to sleep?
Under their covers.

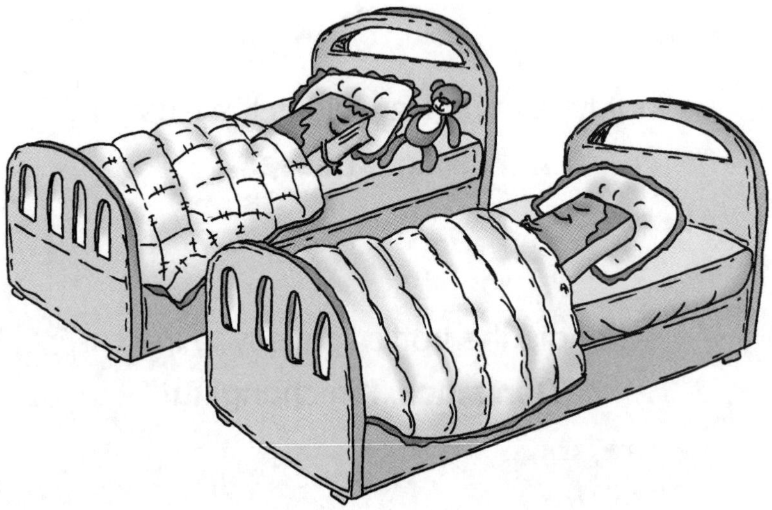

What do you call a man in a red and white outfit who claps his hands at Christmas?
Santapplause.

❖

What do you call James Bond when he's having a bath?
Bubble O Seven.

❖

What do you always get on your birthday?
Another year older.

What do you call a boomerang that doesn't come back?
A stick.

❖

What do you call a pack of wolves?
Wolfgang.

❖

What do you call two robbers dressed in ladies' underwear?
A pair of nickers.

❖

What do you get if you cross a chicken with a cement mixer?
A brick-layer.

❖

What's a top night out for a geologist?
A rock concert.

❖

Why is Santa a good gardener?
Because he likes to hoe, hoe, hoe.

What do you get if you cross a kangaroo with a sheep?
A woolly jumper with pockets.

What do you get if you cross a snake with a builder?
A boa constructor.

❖

What do you get if you cross Count Dracula with Sir Lancelot?
A bite in shining armour.

❖

What do you get when you cross a skeleton with a detective?
Sherlock Bones.

What has a bottom at the top?

Your legs!

❖

Who works at MI5 over the Christmas holidays?

Mince spies.

❖

What sits in a pram and wobbles?

A jelly baby.

❖

What sits on the seabed and shakes?

A nervous wreck.

❖

Why are Christmas trees like clumsy knitters?

They both drop their needles.

❖

Why does a milking stool only have three legs?

Because the cow has the udder.

What type of stories does the sea captain tell his children?
Ferry stories.

❖

What wears shoes but has no feet?
The pavement.

❖

What's pink and fluffy?
Pink fluff.

❖

What's blue and fluffy?
Pink fluff holding its breath.

❖

What did the lovestruck stamp say to the envelope?
"I'm stuck on you."

❖

What's brown and sticky?
A stick.

What do you call a man with a purply-browny-yellowy mark on his forehead?
Bruce.

❖

What happens when Father Christmas gets stuck up the chimney?
He gets Santaclaustrophobia.

❖

Did you hear about the washing-line robbery?
Two pegs held up a pair of pants.

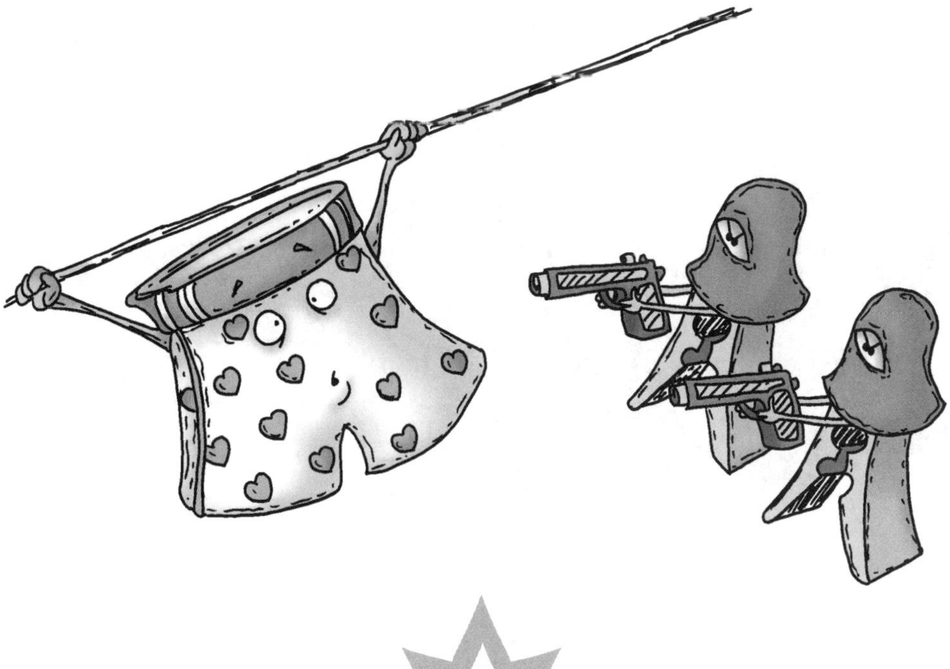

What did the carrot stick say to the home-baked crisp?

"Want to go for a dip?"

❖

When is a car not a car?

When it turns into a garage.

❖

Where can you always find diamonds?

In a pack of cards.

❖

Who pulls Santa's sleigh when the weather is wet?

Raindeer.

What's the difference between a well-dressed gentleman and an exhausted dog?
One wears a posh suit and the other just pants.

❖

What's the difference between a crossword whizz and an old lady with a sweet tooth?
One is a good puzzler and the other is a pud guzzler.

❖

What do you get if you cross Father Christmas with a duck?
A Christmas quacker.

❖

What makes a ringing noise when they come through Santa's letterbox?
Jingle Bills.

❖

What's the name of the country where reindeer run round and round in circles?
Lapland.

What stays in the corner, but travels all around the world?
A stamp.

❖

What's round and dangerous?
A vicious circle.

❖

What has a long tail, colourful feathers and wears a bow?
A birthday pheasant.

❖

Where did the king keep his armies?
Up his sleevies.

❖

Which part of a mermaid is the heaviest?
The scales.

❖

What did the big candle say to the little candle?
"You're too young to go out."

What's green, has four arms, four legs, two heads, two trunks and goes, "Bleurgh!"
Two seasick holidaymakers.

❖

What sound do hedgehogs make when they hug?
"Ouch!"

❖

Where does Tarzan buy second-hand underpants?
At a jungle sale.

Why did the man wear a banana skin on each foot?

He wanted a pair of slippers.

What did the sink say to the leaky tap?

"You're a drip."

❖

Which is the tiredest part of a car?

The exhaust pipe.

❖

Why are elephants all wrinkly?

Have you ever tried to iron one?

What has four wheels and flies?
A garbage truck.

❖

What do you call a judge with no thumbs?
Justice Fingers.

❖

Why are refuse collectors miserable?
Because they're always down in the dumps.

❖

What do plumbers like to go to the disco?
Because they are tap dancers.

❖

Why did the belt go to prison?
Because it held up a pair of trousers.

❖

What flavour squash do monsters slurp?
Lemon and slime.

Why is everyone footsore and weary on 1st April?
Because they've just had a long March.

❖

Why did the boy put his sister under the bed?
Because he thought she was a little potty.

❖

Which flowers grow right under your nose?
Tulips.

❖

What can you always count on?
Your fingers.

❖

A man walks into a bar.
Ouch.

❖

Why was the civil engineer boring?
It was the only way to make a tunnel.

Why did the girl go to school in a helicopter?
She wanted higher education.

❖

Why did the girl take a scooter to bed?
She didn't want to walk in her sleep.

❖

What did Cinderella say when her photos weren't ready on time?
"Some day my prints will come."

Why did the man put his money in the freezer?
He wanted cold, hard cash.

❖

Why don't people watch programmes about origami on television?
Because it's paper view.

❖

Where do cows go to relax?
To the moovies.

Why is a bride like a telephone?
They both have rings.

❖

Why is it expensive bringing up a baby?
Because they are dear little things.

❖

Why was the toadstool invited to lots of parties?
Because he was a fungi.

❖

Did you hear about the two aerials who got married?
The reception was brilliant!

❖

Which is the most musical insect?
The humbug.

❖

What is a dentist's favourite musical instrument?
A tuba toothpaste.

What's the most dangerous sweet in a sweetshop?

A spearmint.

❖

What do snowmen sing at parties?

"Freeze a jolly good fellow..."

❖

What do undercover agents play when they go on a journey?

I spy.

❖

How do you join the girl guides?

Rope them all together.

❖

What is full of holes, but can still hold water?

A sponge.

❖

What's the capital of England?

E.

❖

When do lorry drivers stop for a snack?

When they see a fork in the road.

What did the horse wear at the seaside?
Clip clops.

How do you make a bandstand?
Take away their seats.

❖

What do refuse collectors eat?
Junk food.

❖

How do you turn soup into gold?
Add 24 carrots.

Why do rabbits have fur coats?
Because they'd look daft in leather jackets.

How do you get rid of varnish?
Take away the "r!"

❖

Did you hear about the man who was mad about tractors one day, but bored of them the next?
He had become an ex-tractor fan.

❖

Who stole the sponge from the bathroom?
The robber duck.

What do the letter A and a rose have in common?
Bs come after them both.

❖

Did you hear about the embarrassed toilet?
It was flushed.

❖

Why were the Middle Ages so dark?
Because there were so many knights.

❖

Did you hear about the actor who fell through the floor?
It was just a stage he was going through.

❖

Why did the newspaper blush?
It saw the comic strip.

❖

What did the girl say when she gave herself a haircut?
"It won't be long now."

What did the 8 say to the 3?
Where's your other half?

❖

How did the two cheeseburgers get married?
With an onion ring.

❖

How do dairy farmers add up?
On a cowculator.

❖

I'm reading this book called "A History of Glue".
I can't put it down!

❖

What's taller than a giant?
A giant's hat.

❖

I'm reading another book called "Nuts and Bolts".
It's riveting.

What's the name of a book that tells the life story of a car?

An autobiography.

❖

Why did the boy keep his guitar in the fridge?

Because he liked cool music.

Where do snowmen dance?

At snowballs.

A cowboy rode to the Wild West Hotel on Friday. He stayed three nights and he left on Friday. How?

His horse was called Friday.

❖

What did the jack say to the broken-down car?

Can I give you a lift?

What's the name of a country where every single car is pink?
A pink car-nation.

❖

How do you know when a weaver is telling you a fib?
They spin you a yarn.

❖

What do you get if you cross a cobra trainer and a playwright?
William Snakespeare.

❖

Why did the atoms say goodbye?
It was time to split.

❖

What's the best way to keep a total idiot busy for hours and hours and hours?
Give him a piece of paper with "please turn over" written on both sides.

How did the hermit cover his rent and bills?
Alone.

❖

Why did the break dancer buy a car?
He fancied taking it for a spin.

❖

Why didn't the billionaire use soap?
Because he wanted to stay filthy rich.

❖

What do you get if you cross a cuddly toy with a freezer?
A teddy brrrrr

❖

How did the witch keep her broomstick safe?
With a warlock.

❖

Which part of a turkey has the most rhythm?
The drumsticks.

Did you see the picture of the dangerous and deadly Lone Teddy Bear that was plastered all over the Wild West?

They were wan-ted posters.

❖

Did you hear about the neutron who took a trolley full of shopping to the checkout?

There was no charge.

❖

What did the mother steam train say to the baby steam train at teatime?

Choo choo!

Did you hear about the quad babies?
Four crying out loud.

❖

Did you hear about the jolly fortune teller who wasn't too big and wasn't too small?
She was a happy medium.

❖

Why is an island like the letter T?
They're both in the middle of water.

What's the best way to catch a train?
Follow its tracks.

❖

Where do cars cry?
On the hard shoulder.

❖

Why wouldn't James Bond get up in the morning?
He was told to stay undercover.

❖

What did the letter say to the stamp?
Stick with me and we'll go places.

❖

What do you call a line of Barbie dolls?
A barbeque.

❖

What's full of holes and still holds water?
A sponge.

Why did James Bond have a lie-in?
He was an undercover agent.

❖

What has four eyes and can't see?
The Mississippi river.

❖

How do you put a circus out of action?
Go for the juggler.

❖

Did you hear about the unemployed origami specialist?
His company folded.

❖

How do you make a stiff drink?
Put cement in your cup.

❖

Why did the man give his watch to the building society?
He wanted to save time.

What's green, round and goes camping?

A boy sprout.

Why did the girl disappear into the bowl of muesli?

A strong currant pulled her under.

❖

Did you hear about the firework that was stopped by the police?

They let him off.

❖

Did you hear about the man who found a note on his windscreen complimenting him on his driving skills?

It said, "Parking fine".

What do you get when you cross a film projector
and a swimming pool?
A dive-in cinema.

❖

Did you hear about the crowd of bank robbers
that rushed into the sea?
They started a crime wave.

Boy: "Did you hear about the idiot that keeps saying 'no'?"
Dad: "No."
Boy: "Aha! It's you!"

Who invented the match?
Some bright spark.

❖

What do you call a sleeping Stegosaurus?
A dinosnore.

❖

What language do people speak in Cuba?
Cubic.

❖

How did the lady marry sixteen people in one day?
She was a registrar.

❖

What does the queen do when she burps?
Issues a royal pardon.

❖

What exams do farmers take?
Hay Levels.

Why did the weather forecaster look out of her window first thing every morning?
Because she couldn't see through the wall.

❖

Why did the book spy on people?
It was a peeping tome.

❖

Customer: Can I try on that dress in the window?
Shop assistant: Certainly, madam. But we'd prefer it if you used the changing room.

❖

What did the vegetarian Prime Minister dearly want to do?
Give peas a chance.

❖

Did you hear about the comedian who told his audience he'd run out of gags?
He wasn't joking.

What do you call a deer with no eyes?
No idea.

❖

What goes, "OH, OH, OH?"
Father Christmas walking backwards.

❖

Why was the king so good at drawing straight lines?
Because he was a ruler.

Why did the explorer go to the South Pole?
To visit Aunt Arctica.

What has 50 heads and 50 tails?
50 coins.

❖

What's the richest kind of air?
A gazillionaire.

❖

How do you turn a watch into a stopwatch?
Don't wind it.

What do gardeners read when they're eating their packed lunch?
Weeder's Digest.

❖

What do you get if you cross a satsuma with a stand-up comedian?
Peels of laughter.

❖

Why is it very tricky to open a piano?
All the keys are inside.

❖

How do Swedish people dress in winter?
Quickly.

❖

What is red and yellow and pink and green and orange and purple and blue and black and white and brown?
A box of colouring pencils.

Why was the bass guitarist arrested?
He got in treble.

❖

What do you call a man who's covered in cat scratches?
Claude.

❖

Why were the corduroy pillows in the news?
They made headlines.

❖

What are fortune tellers' favourite plants?
Palm trees!

❖

Why did the toadstool move house?
It didn't have mushroom.

❖

Why did the sleepy boy do laps of his bed?
He wanted to catch up on his sleep.

What did one Venus fly trap say to the other Venus fly trap?

Time's fun when you're having flies.

❖

What tree never grows?

A lava tree.

❖

Why couldn't the girl daydream?

Her mind kept wandering.

❖

Why did the peach go out with the raisin?

Because he couldn't find a date!

How much did the American pirate pay to get his ears pierced?

A buck an ear.

❖

Why did the King go to the dentist?

To get his teeth crowned!

❖

What do you get if you cross a fairytale character and a treasure chest?

Sleeping Booty.

What did one snowman say to the other snowman?
Smells like carrots.

❖

What do you call a little fish that isn't potty-trained yet?
A tiddler.

❖

Which type of tree is invited to the most parties?
The Poplar tree.

❖

What goes out but never comes in?
A candle.

❖

What can you catch but never throw?
A cold.

❖

What is hard to beat?
A bongo drum with a hole in it.

Can a jam jar dance?
No, but a tin can can!

❖

Is it a good idea to swim on a full stomach?
No. It's much better to go to a swimming pool.

❖

What did the boy scout say after he fixed the horn on the toy car?
Beep repaired!

❖

Did you hear about the dastardly thieves who stole all the toilets from the police station?
Detectives have nothing to go on.

❖

What did the two famous composers take to the supermarket with them?
A Chopin Liszt.

Why was the painting sent to prison?

Because it was framed.

❖

William Shakespeare walks into a cafe.

"Hey, you!" shouts the waiter. "You're Bard!"

❖

What's tall, grey, spiky and runs around a prison?

The prison wall.

❖

What do you call a large rectangle of wood with nothing to do?

Board.

Did you hear about the boy who went to buy a camouflage jacket?
He couldn't find one.

❖

What did the egg say to the electric whisk?
I know when I'm beaten.

❖

Why did the farmer bury his money instead of putting it in the bank?
He wanted to make his soil richer.

How do ancient Egyptian monarchs travel?
By Pharaoh-plane.

❖

When is a racing car not a racing car?
When it turns into a pit lane.

❖

Where is Captain Hook's treasure chest?
In his treasure shirt.

❖

What sound does a steam train make when it has a cold?
Aaaaah-choo-choo!

❖

What did the rug say to the wooden floor?
Don't worry. I've got you covered.

❖

What type of pants do storm clouds wear?
Thunderpants!

Did you hear about the boy who had to visit the doctor after swallowing all of his pocket money?
There's no change yet.

❖

What do you call a flying police officer?
A helicopper.

❖

What's the cleverest car in the world?
A Smart car.

❖

Did you hear about the man who didn't use the letters E, F, O, R or T?
He couldn't spell for toffee.

❖

What's conjunctivitis.com?
It's a site for sore eyes.

If the orange house is on the left side of the street
and the purple house is on the right side of the street,
where is the white house?
Washington, DC.

❖

Why couldn't Batman go fishing?
Because Robin had eaten all the worms.

❖

What do you get if you cross Batman and Robin
with a steamroller?
Flatman and Ribbon.

Which computer will keep you dry in the rain?
A Mac.

❖

Did you hear about the bad-tempered boy who lost one shoe?
He was hopping mad.

❖

Did you hear about the criminal wearing a camouflage suit whose shoelaces were tied together?
He could hide but he couldn't run.

What did the two-storey house say to the one-storey house?
Bung-allo-allo-allo.

❖

What's the hardest thing about learning to ride a bicycle?
The ground.

❖

How do you teach a baby car to drive properly?
Work on its motor skills.

❖

Did you hear about the girl who was bopped on the head by the frisbee?
She wondered why it was getting bigger and then it hit her.

❖

What was Camelot?
The place where King Arthur's Egyptian friends parked their camels.

What do Norwegians drive?
Fjord Mustangs.

❖

Did the secretary file her nails?
No, just the paperwork.

❖

If two wrongs don't make a right, what does?
Three lefts.

❖

Why does the statue of Nelson stand on top of Nelson's column?
Because it can't sit down.

❖

Did you hear about the unemployed court jester?
He was no one's fool.

❖

Why are oil rig workers so sleepy?
Because drilling for oil is boring.

What happened when the boy with no jokes announced he was going to be a stand-up comedian?

Everybody laughed.

❖

Did you hear about the little old lady on the zebra crossing with super-human strength?

She could hold up traffic.

What kind of vehicle gets the hiccups?

A hiccup truck.

❖

Did you hear about the letter O that kept gnashing its teeth?

It was a vicious circle.

❖

What was Robin Hood's mum called?

Mother Hood.

❖

Why did the girl spray her alarm clock with insect repellent?

It was full of ticks.

Why couldn't anyone telephone the launderette?

Because there was nothing on the line.

❖

Why did Robinson Crusoe say "Goodbye" on Thursday?

Because he was leaving Friday.

❖

What starts with P and ends with E and has thousands of letters in it?

Post Office.

❖

Which king had a numb bottom?

The one who was longest on the throne.

❖

Why did the owner of the cake shop laugh?

Someone tickled his fondant fancy.

❖

Why wouldn't the bald man lend anyone his comb?

He couldn't part with it.

Why did the toilet paper make a dash down the hill?

It wanted to get to the bottom.

❖

Do you want to hear a long joke?

Jooooooooooooooooooooooooooooooooke.

❖

What do you call a fairy that stands in cow dung?

Stinkerbell.

❖

How can you make your money go a long way?

Put your piggy bank in a rocket.

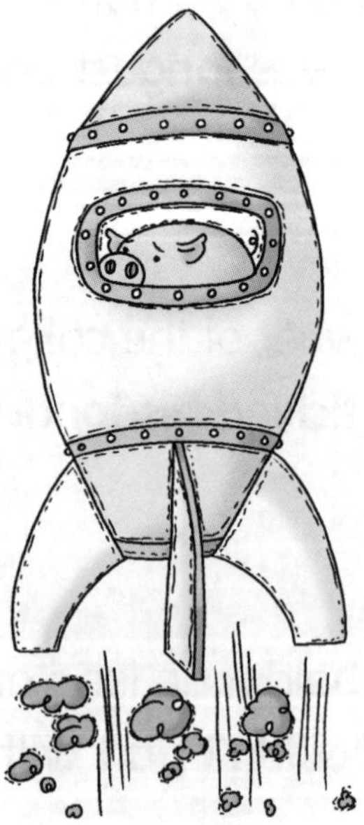

Why didn't the top salon stylist cut hair any longer?

Because she cut it shorter.

❖

What do you call an incredibly polite person who builds bridges and lays roads?

A civil engineer.

❖

Where do you find a giant scholar?

Around the neck of a giant's shirt.

❖

Where do candles go to learn to be celebrity popstars?

Flame Academy.

❖

In a family with seven children, why was the youngest late for school?

The alarm was only set for six.

❖

Why does a tricycle stand up on its own?

Because it isn't too tired.

What's the quickest way to make a fire with two sticks?

When one of them is a match.

❖

What did Picasso eat for breakfast?

Surreal.

❖

Are thieves right-handed or left-handed?

Neither. They're red-handed.

❖

Why do magicians have such dainty fingers?

Because they're sleight-of-hand.

❖

Why couldn't anyone telephone the bride-to-be?

Because she was engaged.

❖

Why do businesspeople carry umbrellas?

Because umbrellas can't walk.

Did you hear about the man who parked his car
in a tow-away zone?
When he got back, the whole street was gone.

❖

Why couldn't the sailor's knot and the angler's knot
go ashore and have some fun?
They were all tied up.

❖

What did one Arctic explorer say to the other Arctic explorer?
I'd hate to have a bear behind in this weather.